An Advertiser's Dream

HEADLINES
That Work

How to Get the more Results from your Ads Now

Le David Morris

How to Get the More Results from your Ads

Published by
Heraldry Publications
18 Sanders Rd, Building 2
Humboldt, TN 38343
Phone: 731-499-3815
Website: www.morrislrd.com
Email: morris@click1.net

ISBN: 13:978-0615865812
ISBN: 10:061586581X

Acknowledgements

This book is dedicated first and foremost to my loving and supportive wife, Deborah L. Morris who has spent numerous hours proofreading and editing the manuscript which generated this book.

And Dedicated to the Memory of

Dr. Dalton B. Jones an extraordinary role model in the advertising industry.

How to Get the More Results from your Ads

PREFACE

Doing It Wrong

I am not a philosopher nor do I lay claim to being wise or being smart, but what I hope to do is share some things I have learned, much by accident and even more through the wrongs and errors that I have practiced as rigidly as if they were the gospel truth.

I proliferated these wrongs and errors as simple mistakes because I did not want to admit how wrong I was. I fall victim and I am guilty of this miserable malfunction. This book is a feeble attempt to compensate and excuse those grievous errors, and help young writers to avoid this trap where I feared to face life honestly and openly.

Philosophy is derived from two Greek words, Philos (the love of) and Sophia (wisdom), or "The love of wisdom." The least any writer can hope is that we learn from our mistakes. That is what I have come to believe and just maybe I am a little wiser because of it.

How to Get the More Results from your Ads

King Solomon was such an advocate of the love of wisdom that he petitioned God for a greater portion of wisdom. He recognized that many were falling victim to the vague and mysterious, rather than keeping it real, or using common sense. People would adhere to the esoteric or deep and profound.

In his wisdom he discovered that exposing what it was that, "Doing It Wrong," provided the solution being real or doing it right. Thus, you have the famous dialogue of where Solomon tells the two women, no problem, we will simply cut the baby in half, and give each of you half.

He knew the solution was ridiculous, but he also knew that the real mother would surface and that the wisdom of common sense would prevail. When looking at headlines we may have to look at, "doing it wrong," in order to do it correctly.

The advocates of the cute or funny commercials, just to be cute and funny, and drawing attention to themselves is an extreme disservice to advertising or promotional messaging. When the headline calls you, excites you or provokes you to read on until you make a decision to buy or purchase the product or offering, then it is real and you can make a wise decision.

HEADLINES That Work

The Good, the Bad and the Indifferent

Before I was a freelance copywriter, I worked as an ad-man for a small local magazine in the Greater St. Louis area. I learned about advertising while there. Actually, I had been indoctrinated to the concept from one of my college professors at Southern Illinois University – Edwardsville. Doctor Dalton B. Jones was an outspoken retired ad man from a previous generation. He made the thought of advertising come alive in the hearing and visualizing of his students. Excitement toward ad copy oozed from every word that protruded from his lips. We were mesmerized with his hypnotic utterances.

When completing my obligation with the United States Air Force I had a vague idea that I wanted to become an aeronautical engineer, but I had very few assets other than through the G.I. bill and the state of Illinois veteran scholarship. An inventory of my former grades and financial availability meant I was limited to a state college or university. I could live at home practically free and go to a local college or university meaning my two choices were to go to Southern Illinois University at Edwardsville or Belleville Community College. I chose the university route thinking that I could complete all of my pre-engineering courses the first two years and transfer the last two.

I was not committed to this plan or any plan. I wavered, or perhaps floundered, from major to major changing my major to physics, then math, accounting, then to business, and finally to advertising and marketing. (Changes in the school of business were easy to do without sacrificing too many credits.) Up to then I was not satisfied with each change. I can not tell you why my hesitancy led me to discover, to my surprise, that I would come to enjoy advertising classes.

I am indebted to Professor of Advertising Dr. Jones. He had a big influence in the direction my life would take, or what it would mean to me as a freelance copywriter today. He was more than a teacher. He was a mentor, a counselor, friend, and later became a co-worker. Dr. Jones was helpful in permitting me to start working as an ad-man over thirty years ago. An ad-man is what is known as a copywriter today.

Dr. Jones was very stern in his opinions. His class began at 7:00 AM, giving us working students time to be at work by 9:00 AM. His favorite sayings, in reference to advertising were - "it is not necessary to reinvent the wheel, if it ain't broke, don't try to fix it, and much of what you do in advertising was used successfully by P. T. Barnum in the mid-1800s."

I told Dr. Jones I really enjoyed his class. It was no accident that when an advertising position opened, he recommended me for the position. What I did not know was that in addition to preparing the ad copy, I would be responsible for securing new advertisers. Calling on businesses and selling advertising space would become a priority. At first I was somewhat reluctant to call on prospects, but after a few attempts I started looking forward to meeting the next potential prospect. Each customer was unique and very interesting. These clients helped making the transfer easier than I expected. Each customer made me feel that I helped them with my suggestions.

The next challenge to me was that the ad-copy the magazine was using was not only boring, but really stunk. According to Dr. Jones methodology and in his words, "it was dead display ads devoid of life and needed to be put out of its misery." In the beginning the publisher and editor did not want to bother the customers with changing their ad copy. After all it was the same kind of ads that were found in most media of that day. Very cautiously management gave me permission to approach clients with benefit balanced ad copy.

How to Get the More Results from your Ads

As mentioned previously the clients treated me with respect. They saw I was attempting to help them. Most of them had never heard of benefit balanced advertising, but were hoping for improved results. I believed Dr. Jones had made this term up. I shared with them that this was a new trend in advertising that a lot of others were using, and it was working in various areas in the country. One client designed and built custom bicycles. His shop reported a surge of new bicycle buyers pleasing him immediately. We were able to convert his eager testimony into many sales. I was glad because I was receiving commissions on new and larger ads being placed by these business owners and by new customers. The next few years were great. The income was good, and the position seemed wonderful.

I became restless and began looking for other opportunities. Even though I enjoyed what I was about to do, my job choices were shifting greatly. I received an offer from a photography company doing church directories. The career paths I chose led to many jobs and career directions from a call to ministry, to teaching engineering, architectural and graphic design in a high school and local college. I had the opportunity to use my copywriting skills. I began a screen printing business fifteen years ago which has drawn on my copywriting skills in creating catalogs, booklets, flyers, brochures and advertising copy. I also have secured freelance assignments over the years.

Desktop Publishing and Design

While serving a church in Memphis I had surgery for colon cancer. As I recovered I learned to use several graphic design software programs, and two word processing programs to pass the time. The old method of cutting and pasting by hand became obsolete. Desktop design and publishing became delightful for me. Email and web copy development became the new challenge. As I learned I did not realize how crucial these devices would be enhancing my toolkit today.

My first attempt at desktop publishing was on a Commodore 64. To create a four page brochure (5.5" x 8.5") one had to create each page individually, cut the pages out one at a time and glue or tape them together to get front, back and the two inside pages. Later clipart was introduced to the computer. Originally it was still done by cutting and pasting manually. Later when moving to an IBM clone I was introduced to WordPerfect which offered landscape and column design. I then moved to booklet design and on to formatting books. Mi-

cro-Soft Word and other word-processing programs have come a long way. I have just discovered
Open Office, a free program you can download
online. I am learning its formatting features as I
type this book.

From Ad-man to Freelance Copywriter

When I began my career writing copy for a local
magazine the prevalent term was ad-man. Although there were women entering the business as
ad-women. Later the term ad writer became dom-
inant. As I went out on my own the appropriate
term was independent ad writer. I was not aware
of the term freelance copywriter until I read Peter
Bowerman's book, ***The Well-Fed Writer***, 2010.
(I believe he also introduces the term "freelance
commercial writer." pp.2-4.)

I do not possess the skills that many graphic designers have acquired, but my limited experience
has helped me to give seasoned graphic designers
a clearer picture of my vision for many projects. I
have learned that copywriters need to give respect
to the graphic designers with whom they work. A
team effort is imperative in realizing the outcome
of the ultimate product.

When one of my church members retired in the
middle of the year, I had the skills to temporarily

replace him for twenty four years. During this time I assisted the state of Tennessee in developing curriculum for a course in job skills development. I produced brochures for recruiting students in vocational career courses. Additionally, I edited and published four newsletters, and wrote a $25,000 grant for a new computer lab to be used to teach architectural and engineering design and web development. When I received the grant I was required to attend a two week immersion workshop on web site development taught by the state.

The late Mrs. Thelma Barker, a co-worker and friend, introduced me to the wonderful world of email in the late 1980s. I converted one of my monthly newsletters to a weekly email update going out to several thousand readers. I was pleasantly overwhelmed by the results.

In December, 2010 I was blessed by having a stroke. The reason I say I was blessed is the stroke saved my life, because one brave doctor told me if I did not lose weight I was going to die. Before I attempted to convince myself that the 430+ lbs. I was carrying was OK. The six months after the stroke was spent in physical therapy to relearn to walk with a cane and to go on what I call the "fear diet." I was afraid to eat more than a few bites at a time. I shed 95 lbs. very quickly. Today I eat moderately – no more than 2500 calories a day. I am still losing weight, but slowly. I do not recommend the former rapid weight loss unless you are under a doctor's care and observation. I have some minor problems with my right leg, but I am blessed to be able to write the book you are reading today. I am bountifully elated to be alive and reviving my freelance copywriting service.

Table of Contents

PREFACE V

    Doing It Wrong.. V

    The Good, the Bad and the Indifferent vii

    Desktop Publishing and Design.. xi

Chapter One.. 1

    An Introduction to Independent Ad-writing 1

    Born and Bred for Advertising 3

    Stumbled into Freelance Copywriting 5

CHAPTER Two 9

    Secret I - The Key of Attraction 9

    The Story 9

    The Purpose of Headlines... 12

    Screen-printing Success with FREE Offer.......................... 14

    The Grocer's Headline 14

CHAPTER Three... 17

    Secret II - The Key of Attention....................................... 17

    P.T Barnum Advertiser Extraordinaire 17

    Stay-At-Home Mom.. 20

CHAPTER Four... 23

    Secret III - The Key of Attainment................................... 23

How to Get the More Results from your Ads

Who Can Write Capable Headlines 23

80% Will Read the Headlines... 25

The Few Seconds Rule 25

Headlines Do Not Come Easy 26

Headlines Draw You In.. 26

The Call to Copywriting.. 26

Writing for the Internet 29

CHAPTER Five 33

Secret IV - The Key of Approach 33

9 Steps That Influence Headlines to Empower................................. 33

One-Half – Alliteration... 33

One – Improvement – Make It Better... 33

Two – Impact - The Headline Must Influence................................... 34

Three –Infinitesimal - Keep the Headline Short 36

Four - Inclined - Headlines have to Propel Action 38

Five – Irresistible - Action Potent Words... 39

Six – Inventive- Headlines Evoke Inspiration................................... 41

Seven – Invaluable - Headlines Reflect Worth 41

Eight – Impassioned - Headlines Unfurl Emotion............................. 42

Nine - Igniting – Headlines that Generate Excitement 42

Bonus – Intervention – Overcome Obstacles 43

CHAPTER Six... 45

Secret IV Continued - The Key of Approach...................................... 45

26 Headlines – Formulas, Suggestions and Working Models That are
Powerful. 45

ONE: If you're (a frequent traveler,) you can (save 50% on your
travel.) 46

HEADLINES That Work

TWO: (Four) Ways to (lose 30 Pounds in 30 days.)..........................46

THREE: Tennessee Woman Discovers a Simple method to make 1.4 Million Dollars in Six Months With Less Than $15.00 Investment...47

FOUR: Who Else Wants (a Greater Salary?).......................................47

FIVE: THE 10 TOP THINGS YOU CAN DO TO ENHANCE YOUR RETIREMENT. 48

SIX: I lost 213 lbs. Using This Dynamic Method. 48

SEVEN: How (this obvious mistake) made Me (Rich.) 49

EIGHT: The Secret of (writing an EBook.) 49

NINE: Here is a Method that is Helping (business) to (keep more profit). 49

TEN: Warning: (three out of five office workers will lose their jobs in the next five years.) 50

ELEVEN: See How Easily You Can (design a bookcover for publishing your book.)...50

TWELVE: Little Known Ways to (cooling your home and saving money.) 51

THIRTEEN: Do You Recognize the (5) Early Warning Signs of (a Stroke?) 51

FOURTEEN: Get Rid of (This Problem) Once and For All...................52

FIFTEEN: The Lazy (Women's) Way to (Writing a Novel.)................52

SIXTEEN: If You Don't (do it) Now, You'll Hate Yourself Later. 52

SEVENTEEN: Design your own T-Shirts Online Quickly and Inexpensively Using our FREE Templates...53

EIGHTEEN: Here's a Quick Way to (Eliminate an Annoyance) 53

NINETEEN: Now You Can (have Favorable Outcomes) (with Wonderful Results) 54

TWENTY: Making Magnificent and Majestic Proclamations............54

TWENTY-ONE: (Take Action) like (an Authority Figure) 55

How to Get the More Results from your Ads

TWENTY-TWO: Promote the "How-to" Longing 55

TWENTY-THREE: Have a (or) Build a (House) You Can Be Proud Of.56

TWENTY-FOUR: Are You (Wishing You had a Better Job?)..............56

TWENTY-FIVE: What Everybody Ought to Know About (buying classy cloths)...56

TWENTY-SIX: Straightforward or Basic Headlines...........................57

CHAPTER Seven 59

Secret V - The Key of Alignment...59

A Copywriter or an Ad-person..59

Freelancing 59

Going into Business as a Freelance Copywriter.......................62

Jobs-Freelance-Copywriters 66

Places to Work as Freelance Copywriter 67

Local Places for Freelance Copywriters 68

Fees 68

Do not Limit Your Expectations..72

CHAPTER Eight 75

Secret VI - The Key of Audience 75

Marketing 75

Social Marketing 77

Some More Marketing Tips 79

Press Releases 80

Write and Publish a Book 84

Self-Publishing..85

WHO NEEDS YOU 87

Service Organizations 87

HEADLINES That Work

Corporations 88

Associations 89

Large School Districts - Groups - Clusters 89

Colleges and Universities 90

Graphic Designers 90

Events, Conferences and Shows 92

Marketing, PR and Advertising Agencies 93

Finding Clients 94

Prospecting 95

The 30 Second Speech 99

George 101

Selling 105

CHAPTER Nine 107

Secret VII - The Key of Attitude 107

Considerations 107

Beginning the Work through Honest Effort 108

Explore Proximities 110

Courtesy 111

Testimonials and Interviews 112

Hiring an Assistant(s) 112

The Good Client 113

The Bad Client 113

Titles of Articles and Books Speak as Headlines 114

More on Articles 115

Reveal Pertinent Results 117

Anticipate Doubts or Misgivings 118

How to Get the More Results from your Ads

Direct Mail Pieces...118

Personal, Friendly, and Up close 122

Write to a Particular Individual.......................................125

Concentrate on the Greatest Benefit or Value.............126

Sophia's Call 127

EPILOGUE...127

It is Great for Me 128

No Defeats..128

Diversified with Help 129

Both Worlds..130

Copywriting in All Jobs..130

Volunteer Organizations..130

Low Cost Marketing 131

Printing Process..132

Plenty of Work 133

Social Media 134

One out of Twenty Will...135

The Last Two Years...135

Last Words..136

Suggested Reading..138

Chapter One

An Introduction to Independent Ad-writing

A good headline can be thrilling or even spine-chilling. A bad headline will need a funeral director and still does not smell good. An ad-writer or copywriter is one who uses words to create copy for advertising or selling a product or service to buyers. The headline is at the heart or above leading into the body or content of an ad. In my early years I was an in house ad-writer, or what is referred to today as a copywriter. Later on I would become an independent ad-writer or a freelance copywriter as it is known today. An independent ad-writer is one who is self-employed and markets her/his services to clients that employ their services on a per job basis. (Note: I will use the term independent ad-writer and freelance copywriter to mean the same.) Some freelance copywriters are kept on retainer basis to do a variety of jobs.

How to Get the More Results from your Ads

The services of the independent ad-writer include providing many types of copy for products. Essentially the copy creates a mindset that motivates the reader to buy or apply for the offered service. The headline steers the copy into the direction it needs to go. Often the freelance copywriter not only produces copy, but advises the client on many uses and direction for the finished product.

Many clients are very capable to do their own copywriting. They have good grammar skills, and they have intelligent use of words and phrases. They understand what they need to do to produce quality copy. Their dilemma is usually a matter of timing and priority. With cutbacks and companies sustaining a leaner organization they are often forced to outsource things like copywriting. Things that use to be done in house are now done by freelancers and service companies that are only contracted when needed. Their work schedules do not permit them time to do copywriting. The clients benefit from saving on salaries and benefits. The freelancer benefits by receiving projects with which to work.

An independent ad writer can provide a fresh viewpoint, and sometimes provide skills that the client does not have available. She/he brings knowledge to what good copy looks like. Often the freelance copywriter discerns authentic, appealing advertising which will provide the thrust needed to create benefit balanced copy.

In the marketplace, the freelance copywriter is usually equipped with a laptop and ***J.I. Rodale's The Synonym Finder***, paper and a printer. Let me expand the concept that the ***Rodale Synonym Finder*** is the best friend a writer, especially a copywriter, can have. Its massive 1361 pages make it one of the largest thesaurus available.

Basically an independent ad-writer is commissioned with producing copy that sells. A freelance copywriter is self-employed and contracts his services to others to produce copy that assists the client in selling her/his products or services. The freelance copywriter is doubly involved in sales since she/he sells services to enhance the selling of others offerings. The client pays for the knowledge, expertise and finished copy produced by the freelancer. We will discover payment methods in chapter six.

Born and Bred for Advertising

JoAnna is all Southern with the, "Ya'll come back now." She is the youngest of three children. Her older brother is 49 and her sister 47. JoAnna is very pretty in her mid-forties looking more like late twenties or early thirties.

JoAnna excelled all the way from grade school through college. She was singing solos in church at the age of seven. Being well-versed in music, JoAnna had starring roles in elementary school through college plays advancing on to little theater productions. Her continuing talent helped to win many beauty reviews.

Her mother, Miss Louise, saw to it that her daughter never missed an opportunity to sing, act or perform. She was her daddy's pride and joy. Mr. John Robert, known as 'Big Daddy' or 'Jack Bob' published a dozen local community weekly newspapers, ***The Social Circle Magazine,*** and two radio stations. By the time she was 15 she had her own office and worked after school and in the summer in advertising. Her daddy told her, "Headlines were to advertising like song titles were to music."

She graduated from college with a triple major in journalism, English and music. Her daddy placed her in charge of advertising and editor of ***The Social Circle Magazine***. She still had time to freelance and write jingles for TV and radio commercials - power pact jingles, not just cute little sayings. You might say JoAnna is a no nonsense headline advocate, believing that headlines make an impact on the advertising message.

JoAnna uses freelance writers and freelance copywriters to produce articles, ads and promotional materials for her magazine. She uses her talent for creating headlines often.

Stumbled into Freelance Copywriting

Danny barely graduated from high school. He is married to his high school sweetheart. They have three beautiful children. He works at a local dealership selling new cars. He likes his work, but the demands from family and bills have him strained financially.

A co-worker shared a book she had read that gave instruction on how to start a freelance copywriter business for less than $100.00. She claimed that she had been doing this for almost a year, and had been able to pay off her bills. She was planning to take her family on vacation for the first time on Amtrak to New York City.

He read through the night. The book suggested that he develop a web site. He did. It would cost him $3.00 per month. For a few dollars, Danny was able to secure his domain name danny-writes.com He was excited, but knew he was limited in his grammar and spelling skills. He talked about the possibilities of becoming a freelance copywriter with his wife. She reminded him that English was her best subject in school. She promised she would help with proofreading and editing.

Danny worked afternoons and evenings at the car dealer. During his free mornings, Danny purchased two packages of computer inkjet printer postcards to mail to possible clients. He went to the post office to purchase stamps. Several business people were called that he thought would benefit from his new service. In a few months he was caught up on his bills. Toward the end of the year all his debts were paid, and he was facing a financial freedom that was strange.

The freelance copywriting business was providing income possibilities for travel and fun. He could take his wife to dinner and the theater whenever they wanted to go. Now he is faced with the choice of a job he loved for another job he loved equally as well, or stay with both jobs.

Danny had become an expert using headlines. He had discovered that much ad-copy and promotional materials was good except for the headlines. Many headlines missed their target. Some were funny, some really advertised the business name, but failed to encourage the reader to take the next step to read further. Danny had developed a keen sense for good headline material. His expertise has endeared him to his clients

Which of the above individuals would you pick to help you with your headlines? The answer is...?

Either of the above have developed the skills needed to create good headlines. First, this book is to direct your attention to good headline use. Secondly, this book will attempt to show what it means to be a good freelance copywriter. Thirdly, this book will attempt to take care of and recognize things you need to do to start your business. A passion for good headlines should unfold in the book should unfold as follows.

How to Get the More Results from your Ads

CHAPTER Two

Secret I - The Key of Attraction

The Story

It's Friday! The home phone rings at 6:59 AM. You ignore it as each ring interrupts the glorious, pleasant thoughts of how great it is going to be for you and your family doing nothing but linger on Myrtle Beach, listening to the ever gentle rolling waves and enjoying the sun coming up as golden droplets of spray dance across the shores each time a peaceful wave blissfully approaches the shoreline. Your wife can't stand by and let it ring, because she is a devout believer that every call needs to be answered. It does not matter that you had been planning this get-a-way for months.

All of a sudden you hear this almost teasing sweet voice, "honey it's for you." You can't believe it, no one calls you on the house phone anymore. Your wife says, "The caller apologizes, she said she tried calling your cell phone, but you didn't answer." You yelled back, "I didn't because when I put it on the charger last night, I turned it off believing no one, not anyone, would call at this ungodly time.

My wife shouted back, "she says it's an emergency." I mumble, "who is it—what emergency?" The wife shoots back with a bewildering tone in her voice, "I don't know. She didn't show up on caller ID."

As you slowly drag your feet to the waiting caller you tell your wife, "I'm coming," mumbling something inaudibly nasty. You say with a forced smile, "Hello, This is..." You hear the caller reply in a voice of desperation and relief, "I need your help. They put this on me last night. I didn't get any sleep, and you are the only one who can help us get out of this stinking mess. Can you help me?"

You innocently asked, "Who is this?"

She answers, somewhat taken back, "I'm sorry, this is Phyllis your former co-worker back in the real 'working' world."

You somewhat vaguely reply, "Nice to hear from you. It's been a while. How are you?"

She says, "I know it's been over a year since you did the last job for us, but we sure could use your expertise now."

You say, "What' cha need Phyllis?"

HEADLINES That Work

She states sternly, "They've pushed up the date for the launching of our newest product and we need a promo piece in ten days, can you do it? The copy will need to be in graphic design by Monday, no later than Tuesday. " She screams, "CAN' YA DO IT?"

You tell her, "Hold on for a minute." Then you turn to your wife rather sheepishly saying, "Would you mind if I take a small piece of work with us on vacation?"

Your wife says, "You usually do. Why would now be any different?" You say to her, "I take that as a yes, that it is O.K." She looks at you with that all knowing smile.

You get back to Phyllis telling her, "I do believe I can manage this project in between other things planned for the next few days, but it will run a little extra for the rush service."

A deal is arranged to produce copy for a six panel brochure. The copy will be completed and faxed to the graphic designer no later than 10 AM Tuesday. Your fee will be $2500.00, or about twice what you would normally charge, because of the rush. You go to your file cabinet and retrieve a couple of similar pieces of work you have completed for other projects. Phyllis promises to fax several photos that show what she believes would look nice in the brochure. She will also email the information to describe the features of the benefits of the new product to you this morning.

The check for the fee will be electronically sent to your checking account. She trusts you because you have helped her out before. You trust her because you use to work for her before your Fortune 500 company let you go through a cut back program.

You go on vacation and you work your rushed project at an umbrella table while the kids and their momma play on the ocean shore. (The following story is true, but the name and location has been changed to protect the guilty.)

The Purpose of Headlines

Headlines are developed with two main purposes: First, to get attention and second, to keep a reader reading. The headline ranks as highest priority in ad development or web site design. Writing a new headline for a previous published ad can revigorate it with power and readability that accomplishes sales and profits.

If it is not doing both of the above, then, you are, "doing it wrong." If it does not pull you into the copy, or at least the next subhead, you are, "doing it wrong." If it does not compel you to buy, purchase or subscribe, you are, "doing it wrong."

The solution is quite apparent. When a customer is shopping, she/he wants to fulfill the wants and desires through buying. The con-artist, high pressure sales person and gimmicky comic are not wanted by fast paced purchasers of today.

The headline creator has to be aware that the prospect demands a straightforward transaction that is appealing and of value. Winning headlines will dynamically draw attention and direct the consumer toward action. A bold example would be "How to Win Friends and Influence People," a headline from the book by the same title created by Dale Carnegie to advertise his seminars and workshops.

The example above draws on the need of people to improve their relationships personally and in business arrangements. Carnegie's headline does more than grab ones attention. One wants to know how it can help me, especially helping me to be better prepared in life. (His book was written several decades ago, but still relates to readers today. I took the Dale Carnegie Course, which is based on the book and previous courses.)

How to Get the More Results from your Ads

The most powerful headline is just one word. That word is FREE. It announces or introduces irresistible promises. FREE means there is no cost nor ties to any gimmicks or qualifications. Merchants know that if they get you in the store or to visit the commercial web site the more apt you WILL buy something or sign up for a service.

Screen-printing Success with FREE Offer

A screen printer offered one **FREE** designed and decorated T-shirt to any business or organization in the community. The ad was part of a flyer hand delivered to 150 businesses, churches, organizations and schools within seven miles of the screen printer. The ad attracted two dozen new customers averaging 25 t-shirt sales per customer. The screen-printed 8.5"x11" 150 flyers were self-made at a cost of $2.50. Each t-shirt cost $3.50. Two part time workers at $10.00 per hour for two hours or $40.00. Total cost equals $130.00. Gross sales were $6250.00. Was it worth it? (The above idea was not unique to me. See Mr. Struthers influence below.)

The Grocer's Headline

Mr. Peter Struthers owned a local grocery store competing with the large supermarkets. He hired several junior high students every week to distribute flyers to the neighborhood on Wednesday afternoons.

Many of his customers were aging and could not get out to shop on a regular basis. They were dependent on their children or neighbors. One elderly lady called and wanted to place an order over the phone saying that her husband would pick it up later.

Mr. Struthers knew this couple well and neither one of them should be driving. Something told him to offer to deliver the groceries. It was not the first time he made this particular offer to other elderly patrons. Thus, sparked the idea about advertising the service in his flyers.

The headline on that week's flyer read in big bold print spanning the top:

FREE DELIVERY

Call Before 3:00 PM

Calls increased and business increased by 20 deliveries that week. By the fourth week deliveries were up by over 100 and sales had increased by 27%. Mr. Struthers would load a panel truck with several young teenagers and flyers. He would drop the boys off at locations near the store. He, or one of his sons, would follow the students to make sure every flyer made it to each house in the neighborhood. (I was one of those students hired to deliver the flyers.)

A Must for Every Headline

Four dynamics that should be in each headline either directly or indirectly are compelling, different, explicit and beneficial. Compelling draws the prospect into the copy and to act now. It has to move away from the same old thing and be slanted in a different direction. It must also hone in on explicit points of information. Lastly, the utility of the benefit must be obviously displayed.

If the above forces are designed in the headline there is an enormous probability that it will do the job. The potential buyer is assured a good payoff whether in print or on website making the experience a worthy one.

CHAPTER Three

Secret II - The Key of Attention

P.T Barnum Advertiser Extraordinaire

P. T. Barnum used headlines in advertising copy in the mid-1800s. He experimented with and developed headlines that influenced the people of his day to attend events he was presenting. Often the headlines were more exciting or titillating than the events themselves. A study of Barnum's use of headlines will aid you in understanding your advertising copy. Barnum realized that many readers did not read, but skimmed the articles and ads in print media. Thus, the essence of the message was presented in the headlines in as few words as possible. The headlines were bigger and bolder at the top of the page.

(The following notes are retrieved from my memory of sitting in Professor Jones Advertising 301 class when he was lecturing on P T. Barnum's take on headlines.)

How to Get the More Results from your Ads

To Barnum subtitles or sub headlines summarized the beneficial details and provided additional support for the audience. Some of the subtitles would offer other extra exhibits of provoking captivation to arouse investigation and to explore other activities while there.

Barnum was a leader inducing one to participate as he motivated them through headlines. The question is, "Do your headlines do this?" If not, you may need a commercial copywriter to join you in the preparation of headlines and advertising copy. You need headlines and advertising copy to promote your ideas, products or services.

Barnum knew a forceful headline increases the chance to be heard in an aggressive market. Your headline needs to grab and tug your customer to ring her/him into the rest of the copy. The most important part of your message is your headlines. [It will give a large part of your energy creating to your headlines.] Copywriters make an effort to advantageously design headlines to entice listeners.

Barnum realized headlines are read first - a must priority. They are larger and usually before the rest of the copy directing ones concentration and guiding them to read further. Headlines draw you into the copy naturally. Many readers will skim from headlines to subheads or subtitles skipping much of the content. Headlines have a distinct likelihood to present your information more fruitfully.

Barnum demonstrated that headlines lead the way. Headlines give readers advance notice. They indicate whether the rest of the copy will be something worth your reading more. They compress the entire meaning of the content in a few words.

According to Barnum headlines give a preview of the copy. They instill desire and entice the reader to keep reading. A good headline gets the reader to want more now! Successful headlines talk explicitly to a market. They present you with fresh opportunities to increase excitement.

Barnum contends that headlines plainly present and serve to introduce whatever follows. As an opening or a lead-in, the role of the headline is to succinctly communicate the essence of the message it precedes.

Barnum effectively explains that headlines and sub-headings reveal key bits of information-often with the added power of emotion. A review of the various headings alone can often provide one with the gist of a given message, which, in turn, makes it faster and easier to understand and remember. When you make it easier for your prospects to read and comprehend your messages, you increase the chances of your own success.

Barnum proposed that headlines permit you to amplify your offering by directing your attention and interest at the outset, by using your most appealing selling point in the headline. If your strongest, most desirable product attribute fails to pull prospects in, surely nothing else you could ever say would do the trick either. Thus, the stronger your headline, the more readers that are exposed to your message and they will continue to read. Create every headline to command attention and inspire interest. The more alluring and irresistible you can make it, the more genuine prospects you'll attract and ultimately, the better results you'll achieve. (Dr. Dalton Jones, Professor of Marketing and Advertising), 1980.

Stay-At-Home Mom

Donna is a stay-at-home mother of two young children. Her ex went out to get groceries and never returned home. Without an income, she returned to her parents big home in a St. Louis suburb.

She applied for several jobs, but had found she did not have any of the marketable skills for which employers were looking. Out of desperation, she went back to the chain hamburger restaurant she worked for while going to high school and junior college. The management had changed, but since she knew a little bit about their operation, she was hired as a part time grill cook for Tuesdays, Thursdays and Saturdays.

It was the breakfast-lunch shift. She got off in the early afternoon and it was less than one fourth of a mile from her parents house. Her mother said she would babysit while she was working.

Donna was walking home from work the first day and stopped by the library. There was a new book in the non-fiction section on how to become a freelance copywriter. She took the book home and devoured it. Catching her interest was the part about how a single mother of two had turned her life around by becoming a freelance copywriter specializing in headline transformation.

The woman she was reading about was from a very lightly populated state out West, but had attracted clients from all over the United States. The next time she was in the library she used a computer to look at this person's website. She did a Google search and found a world of freelance copywriters followed by an exploration of their blogs, websites and forums.

How to Get the More Results from your Ads

It was not long before she decided she could become a freelance copywriter emphasizing headline transformation. With the encouragement from her new friends online, in 2010 she made the leap. Today she lives in her own house not too far from her parents. Her freelance business is thriving and she has inner peace and satisfaction.

CHAPTER Four

Secret III - The Key of Attainment

Who Can Write Capable Headlines

As mentioned above, customers are capable of producing good advertising, sales material and promotional and informational materials. It takes a learning process where one is focused and observant of what effective advertising entails. The headline is the essential element. A caution may arise from the limited availability of their workforce.

As a business owner, manager, leader or corporate executive one could be called upon to produce copy for their organization. Headline development will be the key to create the copy. Acquiring this skill will be useful in many arenas and will permit one to promote sales and improve the bottom line.

How to Get the More Results from your Ads

Headlines creation will lead your potential users to your products or services. They will help your users find their way to you. They will believe your offering and attend to your distinct call. The ultimate draw permits compulsion toward what you make available.

Your initial draw through headlines are the only opportunity you may have. Their presentations drive customers to positive action. Regardless of how large or small the advertising may be, these headlines initiate energy and dominate prosperous industry, organizations and businesses.

What is disclosed in this document will help you design credible headlines. It is a recipe that will assist you in learning the craft. The ingredients listed will apply to a wide variety of promotions and advertising. If you use these ideas it will boost your participation. Advancing these techniques will elevate your writing headlines that work, thus leading to fundamental ad creation.

Copywriters have used these recipes and ingredients to prepare headlines. They have been developed over two centuries. A great or ordinary headline may depend on a single word or phrase. (See essential five below.)

HEADLINES That Work

A freelance copywriter is secured when time constraints limit the ability of the client and her/his staff from completing a project. A copywriter may provide a fresh and experienced perspective in a situation where staffs have been reduced for whatever reason.

Headlines are the first thing you see. The impact made on the reader is paramount and must transform a looker to further explore.

80% Will Read the Headlines

Although 80% of readers will read the headline if it is good, only 20% will proceed to follow through to read the remainder. The drawing influence directs your reader's attention.

Every part of a phrase leads you to the next phrase or statement. The more effective your headline, the greater the chance that your copy will be read to the end.

The Few Seconds Rule

Whether you are advertising a project, or are directing a potential reader to your landing page the headline is essential. I heard a speaker say, "...if you do not capture the reader's interest within the first minutes, you have lost her/him." I believe with the bombardment of information overload today we only have a person's attention for a few seconds. Thus, we are forced to make those few seconds count if we want to gain their interest to read further. (See number three below.)

Headlines Do Not Come Easy

It takes time to produce effective headlines. They are important to selling and worth the effort needed to develop extraordinary headlines.

Headlines Draw You In

Initially they interest you enough to keep you reading and ultimately to make a decision or to take some kind of action. The more you work on headline creation, the more you will benefit from its results.

The Call to Copywriting

The suggestions submitted here will help you whether you are an experienced copywriter, or you are creating ad copy for school, business, agencies, organizations, or for others in whatever capacity of which you are part. Hopefully, you might want to learn to avoid the many mistakes and challenges others have faced. The methods presented here should help you in writing your headlines, or other varieties of media. Namely, blogs, sales letters, articles, advertising, white papers, video copy, landing pages, emails, and web copy.

The freelance copywriter is a professional writer in the broadest sense of the word. She/he puts words together that sell a product or service. With respect to non-profits, a freelance copywriter will often assist with organizational fundraising. The freelance copywriter is more likely to be called upon when a need arises in respect to time and staff shortages.

As a professional freelance copywriter one must view copy as a sales tool and not as something funny. They miss the point when entertainment becomes their product. As more and more commercials take on this end they lose sight of their purpose.

Robert W. Bly starts ***The Copywriter's Handbook*** with this 1982 quote from Judith K. Charles that "A copywriter is a salesperson behind a typewriter. (Bly, p.1. I recommend this book highly.), 2005. Today we would replace the word "typewriter" with laptop. The idea remains the same. Selling or a call to action remains the goal.

How to Get the More Results from your Ads

Bly goes on to say that,

> "For years, a certain segment of the   ad-
vertising industry has been guilty of

> Spinning ads out of whole cloth; they place
> a premium on advertising appearance, not
on   the reality on sales." (Bly, p.4), 2005

Bly again states that

> "...the goal of advertising is not to be liked, to
> entertain, or win advertising awards; it is to
> sell products. The advertiser, if he is smart,
> doesn't care   whether people like his
> commercials or are entertained or amused
> by   them. If they are, fine. But commer-
> cials are a   means to an end, and the   end
> is increased   sales—for profits-- for the
> advertiser." (Bly, p2)

The above may seem clear, but often becomes con-
fusing when we forget the objective of the ad is to
sell. Ads do not have to be boring and they can be
pleasing, but they must sell in order to pay to run
them. Thus, the copywriter is challenged to be both
creative and focused on selling.

Maintaining focus will cause the writer to design
copy that stresses the reason a person would want
to purchase the object being sold. Selling, not

amusement, is the desired result. In order to do that you need to attract buyers and convince them to buy.

Writing for the Internet

The information in this work applies to web sites as well as printed media, especially, with reference to selling. The internet has radically changed the way we sell. People basically are the same, but web tools offer a new outlet for buying immediately. Writing copy retains its goal. If anything is effected, people have shorter retention. They move on to other arenas quicker. Capturing their attention and retaining up-to-date information is important.

The competent computer buyer is seemingly more aware of being conned. Intellectual and emotional content that speaks to them is discerned for its merit. Buyers become impatient more easily and can slip away with just one click. If anything is different, the copywriter understands that purchasers are better prepared to make or not make buying decisions. Regardless, content is paramount.

Ads today that fail to grab and hold attention are dead on arrival. Headlines are key to overcoming potential problems. A bad headline is the pall-bearer taking the ad to the grave. You will not have a second chance before a customer moves on to the next headline, article, or web site. You must gain that great impression at first glance.

The Pathetic Party Clown

George was billed as "Fantastic George the Magic Clown." The problem was that his magic tricks were lame and did not work most of the time. His flyers and his ads in the community weekly were not working well either.

When his tricks did not work well, the kids laughed at him, and the adults became frustrated with him. He was a flop. Donna's mother had hired George to perform at one of her grandchild's birthday party. As usual none of his magic tricks worked (The Donna from above.) Donna was a newbie freelance copywriter and was looking for clients.

She had seen George's pathetic performance. She had also seen his flyer and misdirected ad in the local weekly. She said she might be able to help. He told her, "I don't have a lot of money. In fact, I don't have any. She said, "that's OK, I need the practice."

She told him, "Your act is good, you make children laugh. Isn't that what clowns are supposed to do?

HEADLINES That Work

You can play up the fact that your magic tricks don't work. The fact is your flyer and ad stink. The copy is fair, but the headline and sub headline promise nothing. They just say, "Hire-a-Clown."

Say something like this:

Laugh like You Never Laughed before

You and Your Kids will Have Fun

With George the Numeric and Unmajestic

His fumbled attempts at Magic will crack you up.

Hire George – for Fun

Call 314-555-1212

To set a Date and Time

How to Get the More Results from your Ads

CHAPTER Five

Secret IV - The Key of Approach

9 Steps That Influence Headlines to Empower

One-Half – Alliteration

Notice the use of I-words. Alliteration is a powerful tool to help your reader to recall your content. Use this tool in sub headlines and subtitles.

One – Improvement – Make It Better

What is the primary benefit of your product or services? Another favorite saying of Professor Jones was, "we need to sell the sizzle, not the dead piece of meat that the steak represents." In other words, what information is the reader going to receive? One must never confuse lively, beautiful, believable benefits with dreaded, drudgery of dead features. Even though the features provide the basis for the benefits, it is the benefits that make it "sizzle."

The stress on beautiful, believable benefits can not be underestimated. The greater the benefit the stronger your client will pay attention to your offering. Benefits are the product of features. Do not confuse features with benefits themselves. Features are how products operate. Benefits are the result. Benefits provide meaning and solutions for avoiding agony and to promote joy and happiness. A feature would be this heater provides 15,000 BTUs. The benefit would be this heater will keep you warmer quicker.

Benefits must be the priority when developing the headline, or speaking to a customer's concerns. The strongest should be presented in the headline. Other benefits should be shown in sub headlines or with subtitles.

Combining several benefits into one gigantic benefit promises a greater response.

An example, **How You Can Make $125,000 a Year Designing and Decorating T-shirts.** Thus, enticing one to look at the benefits of considering a screen-printing business.

When composing a headline you will need to consider customers desire fulfilled through benefits. You will achieve the result through understanding how benefits will bring the expected result.

Two – Impact - The Headline Must Influence

HEADLINES That Work

It requires direction toward appropriate hearers and proclivity to the object or offering. Attend to your readers with the essential benefit. The more you are familiar with your readers, the easier it will be to reach them. Knowing your market will cause you to go in the correct direction and your headline will hit the point.

Dan S. Kennedy is one of the most popular self-help writers and the most successful freelance copywriter. He states that,

> "What your headline says and how it says it are absolutely critical... it will melt resistance, create interest and elevate ... status from annoying pest to welcome guest." (***The Ultimate Sales Letter***, p 49), 2011

Google keyword tool is helpful in discovering terms that will direct you toward your audience. By checking headlines in other ads, brochures, sales letters, and web pages, will give indications for what headlines may do for your ads. If an ad lasts more than 90 days in a periodical, there is an excellent chance that it is reaching its goal. Redirecting and rewording such an ad will aid you in designing your message. It is suggested that you compare five to fifteen of these long term ads.

How to Get the More Results from your Ads

Exploring your trade advances you closer to discerning prospective purchasers wants and needs. Studying blogs, forums, conferences, symposiums and where your market meets will bring you nearer to that comprehension. Being aware of another's desire is a powerful tool.

Ultimately you will want a full picture of your likely consumer. You will want to know where they live, their age range, as well their likes and dislikes. If they are similar to you, it is important to know; they will be easy to write. If not, your knowledge of them will assist in your writings. Their agonies and joys are equally desirable and can become easy to write.

Your message has to be contagious and inviting. It has to represent and influence the field it is intended to reach. Thus, the headline must be slanted toward that end.

Headlines directly aimed at a suitable marketplace reap profitable results. Romance writers reach out in the language for the benefit of their potential market.

Three –Infinitesimal - Keep the Headline Short

HEADLINES That Work

Sub-headlines, sub-titles and the adjacent paragraph can provide extension of the headline. Headlines with a word count of 12 words or less is a great goal. Sweet, simple and short will capture attention easily and effortlessly. At first you might want to write 20 or 30 headlines without regard to length, then rewrite the ads with less words, but retain the meaning.

Consider your headline as a two or three second radio or TV commercial. It must convey a concise dynamic theme that entices the reader to learn more. The secret is you have only a couple seconds to make a reality happen. Taking a longer time will render the headline ineffective. Emphasize a short clear thought or idea that pulls or pushes the reader to read further. Your few words drive the audience to view your content.

The short headline elicits consideration speedily. It hones in strongly and rapidly. Swift strikes accelerate a potential customers reasoning and understanding, thus, creating a desire to discover additional information that will relate to the objective. The objective being the decision to buy or join. Brevity is the ultimate goal.

Quick action attracts attention. Convincing your reader at the beginning will influence her/his choice to follow through.

How to Get the More Results from your Ads

Divide an extended headline up into one main headline and as many sub headlines or subtitles as needed. Include only words that are important to the main concept. Dump those words that would deter understanding. Refrain from words that project hopelessness or pessimistic thought.

Kennedy suggests that,

"A good copywriter creates reader friendliness with a number of devices that nurse the reader along – that push, prod, pull, entice, and motivate.

These devices include short punchy sentences and even shorter non sentences. (***TheUltimate Sales Letter***, p. 112)

What about when you have a lot more to say? Kennedy goes on to further suggest that we can,

"Use the First Paragraph as an Extended Headline"

"Think of it this way: In the first paragraph, you sell the recipient on reading your letter; then in the letter, you sell your proposition." (ibid)

Four - Inclined - Headlines have to Propel Action

HEADLINES That Work

Credibility is dependent on it. We can not overstate beyond practical comprehension. It is necessary to keep it believable, simple and compelling.

Believability comes from trust – close friends, those we share experiences with whom we have shared relationships, those we have known for a long time, businesses with whom we have been associated for a long time. An endorsement or encouragement from these enhance believability.

We believe what we know to be true. We accept authority figures and experts to give accurate and credible information. We are more apt to believe those that look like us, speak like us, live like us, go to the same church, belong to the same organizations and adhere to the same philosophies.

Reliability breeds believability and credibility. Satisfactory experience fosters belief. Honesty perpetuates ethical standing and establishes dependability. Make sure every declaration is absolutely true.

Five – Irresistible - Action Potent Words

Unless we have an intellectual mind like Mr. Spock from the Star Trek series, we are emotional. Our perceptions are influenced by our feelings. We seek gratification now based on the way we feel.

How to Get the More Results from your Ads

Words that dominate our emotions point us to instantaneous fulfillment. These words are emotional (see number nine below) and majestic. They provoke a feeling of euphoria assisting the reader's retention. Memories of a pleasant prominent past erupts from embedded thoughts. Some of these include the following:

accelerate, accomplished, achieve, act, announcing, benefit, boast, burn, capture, change, decide, deliver, discover, eliminate, evaluate, excel, finally, free, find, gain, generate, gift, guarantee, head, health, how to, improved, innovate, increased, introducing, launch, learn, love, master, money, motivate, negotiate, new, now, obtain, overcome, penetrate, perform, proven, persuade, prevent, profit, restore, results, retain, save, serve, simplify, solution, succeed, take, teach, transform, unleash, utilize, win and you

Synonyms and derivatives of these words are as effective.

Direct your information to the reader. Let the dialogue speak as if you are talking just to one person. She/he is the one and only receiver of your pronouncement. If she/he gets it, everyone will. Speak with simple single meaning words that bubble with enthusiasm and thrusts your recipient toward finishing the copy and making decisions.

HEADLINES That Work

Six – Inventive- Headlines Evoke Inspiration

We do not have to refrain from moderate natural humor, but we need to restrain ourselves from the funny funnies. We want to maintain interest without seeming contrived. The message must be natural.

Humorous stories take time that a headline can not afford. (See the few second rule and essential number three above) **BUT** they can divert our attention from the purpose of the headline. Humorous situations can present themselves very effectively in the copy.

Seven – Invaluable - Headlines Reflect Worth

Much of advertising is dull and falls short of its goals. Headlines that are vain and misdirected promote the company name or brand. Not that these are not important, but its wastes space and robs the headline of time. The footer or foot line is a more appropriate place for their name, address and telephone number. Many clients are so use to putting their name in the headlines and become reluctant to necessary change.

The single point that most clients and freelance copywriters disagree upon is the company name and branding is important. **BUT** although the name, address and phone number is important as they are, they do not need to take up primary selling space. (See paragraph above)

Eight – Impassioned - Headlines Unfurl Emotion

When the headline speaks to the emotional need it will gain strength. The relief from agony or the enhancement of contentment and gratification is great. The more intense the emotion can be included, the more it will be of interest and attraction. (See number five above)

The emotional draw is what makes headlines work. Without that emotional pull or push headlines become flat and die before they have a chance to influence anything. (If you notice redundancy here, repeating certain points is a good teaching method.)

Nine - Igniting – Headlines that Generate Excitement

Keep the headline jumping, popping, explosive, and exciting. Let the excitement bring joy into the ad writing. Encourage anticipation to ooze from each word and to flow into the subheads or sub topics. Pump the juice until it is bubbling over.

HEADLINES That Work

Bonus – Intervention – Overcome Obstacles

Do not let the fire die, nor permit your mind to get cluttered. Refrain from letting garbage fog your senses. Don't get the dreaded dead to box you in or block your thought patterns.

One of the biggest obstacles a writer can face is overcoming writer's block. There is not any particular method for avoiding writers block. It can be debilitating and obstructive to meeting ones goals. The best remedy is to get your thoughts focused on an entirely different direction. One suggestion is to randomly concentrate on words in a dictionary attempting to maintain ones thoughts on the meaning of each word. Every time I attempt the process it surprises me how a particular word will electrify my process and help me get my thoughts flowing again.

Similar theme to the paragraph above. Replaced the dictionary with the ***Rodale Synonym Finder*** a book with 1361 pages. It is a three pound monster. It is massive. Same drill. Randomly open to any page and concentrate on the words on that page. Suddenly a connection will leap from that page in a way that I never thought and ideas begin to flow. Try it, see if it works for you.

How to Get the More Results from your Ads

There are reports that napping or sleeping will help in clarifying ones thoughts. Activities such as walking, listening to music, reading or writing about something totally different can assist your refocus. It will unblock your mind and rechannel your attention to a solution.

Another resolution for removing obstruction is discussing the problem with a mentor or colleague with whom you trust. The alternative could be a friend or a spouse who is desirous to assist in a non-judgmental capacity. The fresh eye approach can come from anyone from a close colleague group to a stranger. It depends on the person or persons with whom you feel free to converse.

CHAPTER Six

Secret IV Continued - The Key of Approach

26 Headlines – Formulas, Suggestions and Working Models That are Powerful.

You can change the keys words to adapt them to your particular situation. These are not unique to me. Variations of these have been around for over one hundred years. Modifications to these are my attempt to present a jumping point for your headline creation. Copywriters call these swipe files. We all have them and borrow ideas from each other.

Some of these swipe files have been in existence for two centuries. Because they work, they are passed around. You are not stealing these ideas. You will modify them to work for you and your product or service.

Swipe Files

Copywriting, especially headline copy, is sales copy, or a special call to action. There are too many

How to Get the More Results from your Ads

ads in the publications we read. Bly rightly indicates we ignore most of the ads. There are just too many ads to read. (Bly, p. 12ff) Thus, headlines become important in capturing a reader's attention and leading one to further explore.

ONE: If you're (a frequent traveler,) you can (save 50% on your travel.)

Alternate use of this headline addresses a particular type of individual with the first parenthesis, and the beneficial promise to that person in the content or body copy with the second.

> If you're in the Military, You Can Save 33% on the Shopper's Card.

> If You're a Banker, You can receive a 25% discount on our Seminar

> If You Love Movies, You Can Watch Recent Movies for FREE with our Gold Pass.

TWO: (Four) Ways to (lose 30 Pounds in 30 days.)

A variation on "how to" headline.

> Three Days to a Purpose Filled Life

> Five Ways to Make $1000.00 Today

12 Ways to Design a Deck

THREE: Tennessee Woman Discovers a Simple method to make 1.4 Million Dollars in Six Months With Less Than $15.00 Investment.

Readers do not believe sales copy, because of the hype. Much of what they have heard has been untruthfully delivered by a con. True statements are the only solution to acquiring believability.

Jackson Business Discovers New Method for Printing T-Shirts Faster and Cheaper.
Frustrated Carpenter Builds New Tool to Hold Lumber in Place while Constructing Walls.

NOTE: There are a variety of alternatives one may choose to develop a headline. The method you choose may be flavored many different ways. Write several headlines for your project. Then choose the best one to convey the message.

FOUR: Who Else Wants (a Greater Salary?)

Beginning a headline with a phrase "Who Else Wants..." begs the question that assumes the need already exists.

Who Else Wants a Great Inexpensive Automobile?
Who Else Wants a Softer/Harder Bed?

How to Get the More Results from your Ads

Who Else Wants a Better Love Life?

FIVE: THE 10 TOP THINGS YOU CAN DO TO EN-HANCE YOUR RETIREMENT.

We are bombarded by information overload. We do want to know things that are beneficial to us. What we desire is a feeling of tidy and orderly existence. We want to believe we have control in our lives. Thus, headlines that promise things will give that control.

FREE. The Ultimate Guide to Stress-free Living Free Paper to Creating Better Headlines

SIX: I lost 213 lbs. Using This Dynamic Method.

Give a truthful and simple recommendation. A testimonial headline can do two things for you. First, it presents your reader with a third party endorsement of your product or service. Second, it capitalizes on the fact that people like to know what other people say.

"It is Rather Easy, the Best Tool I Ever Used"
"This Book Helped Me. It Can Help You, Too!"
"It's the Unsurpassed Program on Wealth that has Opened My Eyes."

SEVEN: How (this obvious mistake) made Me (Rich.)

Use this structure when relating a personal story. The key to the most effective use of this template is for the two blanks to dramatically contrast, so that the curiosity factor goes way up and people feel compelled to read more.

How a "Wrong Turn" Saved my Life
How a Simple Investment Made Me Wealthy Beyond My Dreams
How Relocating to Tennessee Opened up Better Opportunities for Jobs

EIGHT: The Secret of (writing an EBook.)

"The Secret of..." works. It exposes limited information and evokes possibilities even though it is used often in headline construction.

The Secret of Making your Job Secure
The Secret of Protecting Your Home Against Invasion
The Secret of Obtaining a Low Interest Government Loan

NINE: Here is a Method that is Helping (business) to (keep more profit).

How to Get the More Results from your Ads

The formula is similar to 8 above.

Here is a Method That is Helping Students Learn Math
Here is a Method That is Helping Husbands Keep Happier Wives
Here is a Method That is Helping Writers Find Publishers

TEN: Warning: (three out of five office workers will lose their jobs in the next five years.)

Headlines that use *"warning"* captures interest.

Warning: If Your Company only Sells to one Store Your Future is Controlled by that Store.
Warning: Two Out of Every Three Small Companies Will Disappear in the Next Five Years—Will You Be One of Them?
Warning: Discover The 4 Deadliest Problems Facing Parents Today and How to Prevent Them.

ELEVEN: See How Easily You Can (design a bookcover for publishing your book.)

The quick and easy gains our attention.

See How Easily You Can Use a Digital Printing Press

HEADLINES That Work

See How Easily You Can Buy a Home
See How Easily You Can Attract New Customers to
Your Store

TWELVE: Little Known Ways to (cooling your home and saving money.)

Similar to: "The Secret of..." headline.

Little Known Ways to Profitably Publishing Your
Book
Little Known Ways to Keeping your Home Safe
Little Known Ways to Maintain a Healthy Life

THIRTEEN: Do You Recognize the (5) Early Warning Signs of (a Stroke?)

OK, technically this is still a list, but it's wrapped up in a much more compelling structure than your typical "Top 10" article. People want to avoid problems, and this headline promises the critical tips before it's too late.

Do You Recognize the 5 Early Warning Signs of
Students Ready To Drop out of School ?
Do You Recognize the 7 Early Warning Signs of
Faulty Insulation in Your House?
Do You Recognize the 7 Early Warning Signs of
Drug or Alcohol Problems?

How to Get the More Results from your Ads

FOURTEEN: Get Rid of (This Problem) Once and For All

A classic formula that identifies either a painful problem or an unfulfilled desire that the reader wants to remedy.

Get Rid of Your Weeds Once and For All
Get Rid of a Pesty Gopher Once and For All
Get Rid of That Old Car Once and For All

FIFTEEN: The Lazy (Women's) Way to (Writing a Novel.)

The headline has always worked well with time-pressured people, and that's certainly true for most people today. No one likes to think of themselves as lazy, but everyone likes to save time and effort.

The Lazy Actor's Way to Fame
The Lazy Father's Way to Changing a Diaper
The Lazy Salesperson's Way to Make More Money with Less Sales

SIXTEEN: If You Don't (do it) Now, You'll Hate Yourself Later.

We love to belong, but feeling excluded is a real bummer. Whether it be a financial opportunity or the social event of the year, we simply hate it when we get left out.

If You're not Playing with your Kids Now, You'll Hate Yourself Later
If You're Not at this Meeting Now, You'll Hate Yourself Later
If You Don't Buy Gold Now, You Will Hate Yourself Later

SEVENTEEN: Design your own T-Shirts Online Quickly and Inexpensively Using our FREE Templates.

Derive your headline from your primary beautiful believable benefit.

Your Part-time Job Will Lead to Making a Fortune
Build Your Business Step by Step
Receive One FREE Tire When You Buy Three.

EIGHTEEN: Here's a Quick Way to (Eliminate an Annoyance)

We cherish fast and simple ways to eliminate a pesky persistent hassle.

Here's a Quick Way to Teach Your Son or Daughter to Cook Breakfast
Here's a Quick Way to Train Loyal Employees

How to Get the More Results from your Ads

Here's a Quick Way to Keep your Driveway Clean

NINETEEN: Now You Can (have Favorable Outcomes) (with Wonderful Results)

The headline promises a positive response to a shift or change.

Now You Can Change Your Appearance and Meet More Affluent Clients
Now You Can Influence Massive Audiences With These Five Words
Now You Can have Greater Control Over Your Readers

TWENTY: Making Magnificent and Majestic Proclamations

Men and women are drawn by curiosity naturally. (Sounds like news rather than promotions.)

At Last, Botanists have Discovered these Plants Survive in All Climates and are Lusciously Tasty
Announcing this Discovery was Hidden on a Library Shelf at Yale University for over Sixty Years
Now You Can Have That Car of Yours at Half the Cost

Finally, a Cure for the Crud

HEADLINES That Work

TWENTY-ONE: (Take Action) like (an Authority Figure)

The headline creates the image of being like somebody important.

Sing Like a Rock Star
Wear Fashion Like a Princess
Write Like Steven King

TWENTY-TWO: Promote the "How-to" Longing

How-to headlines interests and satisfies longing to elevate our existence. The key is to concentrate on something lacking and provide assurance that this lacking will be relieved. Make sure the how-to lifts up the outcome. Example:

How to Advance Rapidly in Your Job by Taking This Course

> "How to" or "How" Followed by the Result

> How to lose 15 lbs. in 30 days ... Or your Money Back

How to Make a Mint from 3 Secrets Known Only to the Chosen Few
How to Build Anything with Very Few Tools

How to Get the More Results from your Ads

TWENTY-THREE: Have a (or) Build a (House) You Can Be Proud Of

Appeal to vanity, dissatisfaction, or shame. Enough said.

- Own a Car You Can Be Proud Of
- Have a Job You Can Be Proud Of
- Build a Bridge You Can Be Proud Of

TWENTY-FOUR: Are You (Wishing You had a Better Job?)

These are the same as "Do You" question headlines. They are posed to attract attention with wonder. What if things could be different.

Are You Hiding from Bill Collectors?
Are You Prepared for Emergencies?
Do You Know Enough to Advance at Work?
Do You Make These Six Common Mistakes On Your Taxes?
Gotten a Speeding Ticket Lately? Read This
How Do I Know Which Mutual Funds may be Right for Me?

TWENTY-FIVE: What Everybody Ought to Know About (buying classy clothes)

HEADLINES That Work

These headlines confront you to proceed and completing the attainment of or learn about important information.

What Everybody Ought to Know About Computers
What Everybody Ought to Know About Financing Cars
What Everybody Ought to Know About Plumbing

TWENTY-SIX: Straightforward or Basic Headlines

This basic headline simply proclaims the message. It is not elaborate or complicated. It is pointed and aimed toward powerful, yet simple, promotions where common and well known products or services are rendered.

Jordan Jeans are 25% Off
The Ultimate Business Plan
FREE First Month's Rent

Häagen Dazs Ice-cream 20 oz. size $1.50 off

You're Choice

Having the ability to be able to summarize that copy into headlines is part of the trade. A freelance copywriter has two approaches she/he can choose. Firstly, they can design the copy to follow headlines they have developed. Secondly, they can develop the headline after creating the content. The choice is individualistic. Which way works best for a writer may vary. There are advocates on the side of each method. The optimal philosophy is what feels best for the writer is what she/he should use. Remember you do have the options. Do not make this an issue.

CHAPTER Seven

Secret V - The Key of Alignment
A Copywriter or an Ad-person

A copywriter essentially is a person who can create headlines and simply phrase communication that will equip buyers with awareness, comprehensive, and engaging them. Copywriting methods design writing concerning offerings and/ or services to convince the readers to buy or subscribe. Copywriting is powerful writing that advises and motivates. A copywriter takes charge of communication. A freelance headline writer is a subcategory of a freelance copywriter.

Freelancing

A freelancer is self-employed and presents her/his work to clients per project. The term freelance is used in reference to artistic and writing pursuits, but many different types of work now have a freelance component in the work force.

A freelance copywriter is a self-employed individual working on a variety of projects including coordinating a wide spectrum of work and business. You have all the work that your business would entail. You are responsible for securing new clients, and organizing your activities in an orderly manner.

Not everyone can be a copywriter. Only a few copywriters can stand working the self-employed life as a freelancer. The uncertainty of work can be discouraging. It is necessary to find satisfaction being the responsible force determining direction, control in promotion and advertising. Many understand the process of creating convincing writing, but do not envision promoting their service.

If ad-writing is not exciting, you may not desire becoming a freelance copywriter. You should possess the temperament to shift numerable requirements such as selling, following leads, calling potential business clients and to making out bills to be sent to clients. The time when no new business is coming in can be scary for you. In spite of what could be a problem, you have to write intelligently, focused, and provide an energetic persuasive piece. If you have difficulty editing and proofreading you will need someone to do that for you.

You spend time online or at the library investigating concepts, examining and compiling data so that you can write with insight. The freelance copywriter who is not familiar with the client will have to dig to discover information necessary in fulfilling projects. A crucial essential is to learn a mixture of new information. Desiring to learn new things is beneficial. Few freelance copywriters have to cope with all business elements. The unsureness of projects may dampen ones spirit. You need to possess pleasure from creating proposals and selling pieces considering the task of designing exciting composition.

How to Get the More Results from your Ads

Well-grounded freelancers need to adapt to a broad array of customers. Some customers demand attentive guidance. There are those who require only to be briefly involved in the process. Then you have clients that desire endless updates to promote driving the work to completion. Freelancers enjoy association with clients, but sometime desire being alone to generate their work.

Assurance, up to date and creative development is required, while projecting a productive writing style. A special display of talent is a quality that will reap rewards. Freelance copywriting takes stamina. If you are quick, adaptable, developed, self-motivated and a truly effective writer, perhaps this is your irrestible occupation appropriately awaiting you. You may choose it or let it pass you by and hope for the best

Going into Business as a Freelance Copywriter

A freelance copywriter will require private working space. If at home it needs to be separate from the rest of the house. A spare bedroom, a basement or a room over the garage can be converted into a peaceful office. It needs to be away from interruptions and noise. Otherwise you may need to rent a little office in a bank building, or rent an old storefront that can be converted into an office. You will need a table or desk for your computer. A laptop is deemed a basic necessity because of portability. Also needed is a cell phone and cable internet hookup.

You will additionally require software to create bills that keep records of invoices and work in process.

A voice recorder will be helpful. Get a ***Rodale Synonym Finder***, the best and most complete thesaurus you can purchase. Buy a manual on writing style book like the "***Turabain Manual for Writers.***" Your word processing software should include a good spell and grammar check.

This section is targeted to freelance copywriters writing headlines and copy, but could apply to business owners, managers, writers of books, and leaders of organizations.

You determine what to charge, how and when to collect your fees, whether or not you maintain a staff, and where your office will be. You decide if you are going to accept a job.

Many freelance copywriters use a home office. They do not have a regular staff, but may contract editing or proofing sporadically. Most of the contact they have with clients is over the phone, through email or fax.

A freelance copywriter must have above average working ability. She/he needs to be sure of her/his ability and complete jobs on time. She/he will need to work well under pressure. Business management must be systematized with reference to marketing and professional relationships. Adaptability is a necessity. Self-motivation is absolutely necessary.

HEADLINES That Work

Many freelance copywriters begin as college trained with marketing/advertising degrees. Some develop their skills on the job working in a marketing or advertising agency environment. Others may take courses through organizations such as the American Writers and Artists Inc. (AWAI) Many begin part time while working at other jobs, which could be in the advertising industry, or it may not be. When they feel comfortable to make the break from regular work, or believe they have enough clients, they will become full time.

Freelance copywriters usually do not have a graphic design background. Some may have limited ability with graphic design software. They will need to find an agency with graphic design services or a graphic designer to complete their projects. Otherwise the client will need to find a printing firm that does graphic design or secure a graphic designer for the job.

How to Get the More Results from your Ads

Jobs-Freelance-Copywriters

Copywriting jobs vary. Some specialize in a specific market or several markets in which they become familiar, but most serve a broad range of clients and markets. Many of the more common projects are:

Display Ads

Email Copy

Sales Flyers

Direct Mail Programs

Press Releases

Short Sales Letters

Long Sales Letters

Newsletters

Web Page Copy

Public Relations Programs

Print Copy

Copy for Radio and Television

Book Reviews

Greeting Cards

Coupons

HEADLINES That Work

Point-of-Purchase Materials

E-books

Annual Reports

Printed Books

Technical Writing

PowerPoint Presentations

Speeches

Places to Work as a Freelance Copywriter

Knowing where freelance copywriting opportunities are, it is a little easier to identify where to find assignments. The clients with job offers are many. They include:

Advertising Agencies

Brand Marketing Corporations

Catalog Companies

Healthcare Companies

Newspapers

Magazines

Print and Broadcast Media

How to Get the More Results from your Ads

Public Relation Firms

Radio Copy

Real Estate Companies

Television Copy

Trade Journals

Video Copy

Local Places for Freelance Copywriters

Fundraisers

Grocery Stores

Law Offices

Local Political Campaigns

Medical Offices

Restaurants

Small Businesses

Fees

Setting up fee charges can be a very trying task for freelance copywriters. Options to be considered include honesty about experience. If your years of in ad or marketing agency were an ad-person working with publications for 20 years, you are more seasoned than a beginning writer becoming a free-lance copywriter. The rates will demand a higher rate for the seasoned over the beginner. However, both should be able to find work.

Geographic area, projects and availability of writers play a role in charging fees. Metropolitan regions are inclined to promote richer costs. The category of project and its difficulty has to be carefully heeded. A complicated sales letter will generate a more substantial rate than a brochure. In establishing fees, the extent of your customer base and the number of bidders will have a bearing on the rate charged.

Consider looking at elementary expenses: rent, internet connection, phone bill, utilities, and office supplies. Add up your expenses and divide your billable invoices into your expenses to get an idea about your income to expense ratio.

Clients want to hire the best freelance copywriter for the least fee. Copywriters want a large compensation package based on their experience. It is true that the fee is usually based on experience. Dan Kennedy commands $18,000.00 to several million dollars depending on the client need and market. Those with very little experience or no experience may charge as little as $75.00 per hour or as little as $250.00 per project. A seasoned freelance copywriter will typically charge a $150.00 per hour or from $2,500.00 to $10,000.00 per project. Remember what you pay for is what you get.

A full time freelance copywriter will usually either choose the hourly method or the project method. Most prefer calculating the number of hours they believe it will take to complete a project and charge on the project basis. The process includes determining the following:

One Meeting by Phone or Skype – a few will meet at a client's place of business

Research
Reading and Communication
Needed Interviews
Copywriting Time

HEADLINES That Work

One or Two Revisions

The following rates are given as a reference assuming one is a seasoned full time freelance copywriter. Those with less experience might run a little lower. Likewise, those on the upper end will run a lot higher. Remember, these are estimates. Actual pricing may be different.

Brochures	$300 - $1200
Email Copy	$600 - $1200
Flyers	$200- $1200
Journal Articles	$1250 - $3000
Long Sales Letters	$1500-$5000
Newsletters	$200 - $900
Proofreading or editing	$60 - $150
Short Sales Letters	$750 - $2000
Short Essays	$200 - $400
Press Releases	$200 - $600
125 Page Book	$15150 - $27000
200 Page Book	$25000 - $45000
Web Page Copy	$350 - $900 per page
White Paper	$3000 - $7000

How to Get the More Results from your Ads

Hourly $150/per hour

The fee you charge is dependent on experience and expected results. Is it going to be used once or many times and in different ways? Dan S. Kennedy is giving instructions to potential clients on paying fees when he states,

> **"You do not want to overpay but you don't want to underpay either.** You can find, for example, copywriters who'll do a four-page sales letter for $500.00, $5,000.00, $15,000.00, or $50,000.00.   Which is the right fee? It depends on many   factors..." (***The Ultimate Sales Letter***, p. 173, 2011)

Do not Limit Your Expectations

Much of my personal independent ad-writing experience has been experienced from rural West Tennessee and West Kentucky. Nashville is 120 miles from where I live, Memphis is just 80 miles, but millions of businesses are just an arm's length away. They are found on my laptop. Many of my clients are small manufacturers, school districts, doctors and lawyers. The largest of my clients are the state of Tennessee and a few businesses that cater to educational institutions.

The point is you do not have to be limited to your surroundings. The world is at your fingertips. You are only limited by your imagination. In addition to the computer, emails and cell phones are important contact instruments. Some of my best clients are found in small and mid-size towns. The amount you charge is up to you. If you offer a fair service for a fair fee and do good work, you will receive a good amount of work. You will be recognized for the way you complete a job and the quality of your projects. I have specialized in reworking headlines. It has worked for me.

How to Get the More Results from your Ads

CHAPTER Eight

Secret VI - The Key of Audience Marketing

Creating a blog or website to display samples of your work is essential. The work known as your portfolio should depict a variety of work, especially, if you specialize in a particular marketing area. You still have to show how to service that market. Examples would be equipment sales for embroidery and screen printing. Comprehension of the language specific to that industry is absolutely essential. Exposure on the internet saves time when clients ask to review your portfolio.

Peter Bowerman insists that you are marketers that help others promote their products or services, but you must market yourselves to potential clients. He says,

> "This business is, first and foremost, a sales and marketing venture... Remember, in this

business, you are the product, and when you're selling you and what you know you do well, it's a whole other ball game." (***The Well-Fed Writer***. p.17, 2009.)

A basic aid in marketing is forming a peer group of freelance copywriters. The suggestions from such a group will help with sharing crucial ideas in marketing, pricing and other needed information. Within the framework of on-line forums geared toward freelance copywriters, you will discover such a group of individuals who can contribute greatly to your understanding as well you adding your input. You might even develop leads for specific projects. Freelance copywriters become overwhelmed and blessed with an abundance of projects and are delighted to share with their friends. They end up sharing with others they know and respect. You might have the opportunity to share when you become overloaded or you might receive projects when they are facing a tremendous overload.

Social Marketing

It goes by a variety of names, but is recognized as the fastest way to market your product or services. As a freelance headline copywriter you can gain many followers, tribes, circles or friends that can influence the amount of your work. Paula Peters calls it, "online social network," and it is often referred to as social marketing. (***The Ultimate Marketing Toolkit***. p. 93.)

Jason Matthews proclaims that social media is absolutely essential before one is ready to launch a new eBook or printed book. He says: "Before you run off to create and upload eBooks (and I might add printed books), you'll be wise to first develop a social media network and online platform." (***How to Make, Market and Sell Ebooks, All for FREE***, p.15.)

What is about to be revealed is one of the miracles of marketing today. One might ask what that might be. It is the miracle of social media. The following is a true story: A 26 year old woman has been writing books since her late teens. Every book she wrote was turned down by the New York publishing houses. She has discovered Kindle Books by Amazon.

She began a self-publishing process with the help of Kindle by Amazon. As of March, 2011 she had sold over 900,000 Kindle Books and was approaching close to $1.5 million dollars. The question is how did the miracle happen. It was discovered that she had to market her own books, but they could be ordered through Amazon.com. It was advised that social media would be of benefit in the marketing process.

The use of social media to market her books was essential. The work was like a regular job. She used social media about forty hours a week. It paid off. Today she has self-published over 27 books, her income is over 2 million dollars. (I gathered this information from **_You Tube_**, February, 2011 – Au-

HEADLINES That Work

gust, 2012. Several books that I researched suggested using social media. Information about Amanda Hocking's rise to fame is taking the writing world by a storm. (It has made an impact on this writer.) The following are examples of social media:

www.twitter.com
www.facebook.com
www.googleplus.com
www.linkedin.com

Some More Marketing Tips

Marketing is about enduring and influence. This takes persistence especially when new. Clients do not realize they need your service or that they need you to provide that service devotion. The great thing is that these items do not have to take large amounts of time. You make progress when you need occasional perseverance to keep the word out about your service. Assuming people like it, a buzz will generate from happy clients who will actually help with the marketing referring you to others.

How to Get the More Results from your Ads

The term freelance copywriter is becoming popular as more clients desire to experience and use the freshest writers who haven't been discovered by the mainstream public. While it is true that some freelance copywriters are not good (to put it mildly), it's also true that there are many excellent ones waiting to be found. Fortunately, there are many websites featuring these services.

Press Releases

Press releases provide an avenue for your service or your book, and bouncing links to your sites. There are many web sites that have good press release services at no charge, and you can even submit a modified press release to a few different ones. The sites will each have more specifics on how to write a press release for that particular site. Some general things to remember are that these are not supposed to sound like advertising hype; they're meant to have the ring of news copy, what's taking place, and why it is news.

HEADLINES That Work

Submitting a release that reads, "I just wrote an awesome service and everyone try it because..." is not going to be accepted. Likewise, each site contains their own set of rules similar to Ezinearticles.com (listed below). Press releases should answer the questions of what, when, how and why this matters, and not be a big sales presentation.

Here are some web pages that offer free press releases:

1888pressrelease.com
Free-press-release.com
PR.com
PRlog.org

Write and Submit Articles

You may write a book, or you may want to publish short articles online. These can be articles about your book, and your services or any other subjects. Like press releases, submitting articles is a great way to get your name and web site known. Remember to keep your standards high when writing articles and have them polished and of quality content.

Then send your articles anywhere you can get them published without cost. You can even submit similar articles to multiple places, with alterations to each in the title and the first sentence or paragraph to help distinguish them. Here are some great web sites, and again more can be found with the search engine www.bing.com or www.yahoo.com:

http://www.dropjack.com - a place for brief descriptions and links to your web site. They only take a short paragraph so it's more like writing a headline. It will help bring traffic to your web site. http://www.ezinearticles.com - Authors share articles. The site takes a little time and is strict on following their rules for accepting articles, but is really a good place once you get used to it. Your article must be strong and not promotional. If your articles are denied, they will inform you what to change until you get approved.

HEADLINES That Work

http://www.goarticles.com - the self-proclaimed largest free content article directory. I really like them in that the articles post fairly quickly, usually within 48 hours, and they aren't too particular with required criteria. Once online it is sent as does E-zines' and Idea Marketers.

http://technorati.com - A great place in which to submit. These articles you can use on your web site or blog. Thus, they can have a dual purpose to help develop a reader base and can really drive traffic to your websites. They are very choosy in their article choices and you will have to go through the process of getting approved to write for them first. When selected you will be delighted that your articles will get picked up by other online magazines. It is ter-rific in that your web site address is sent by other people. It is as if someone else is working for you at no cost.

How to Get the More Results from your Ads

Write and Publish a Book

Same as above recommendations about publishing a book or eBook. Additionally, the following advice from several people including Dan S. Kennedy and Matt Zagula suggest you write a book. It enhances and creates trust and authority. In their words,

> "There is no more essential tool of authority than authorship." (***No B. S. Trust-Based Marketing: The Ultimate Guide to Creating Trust in an Understandable Un-Trusting World*** by Dan S. Kennedy and Matt Zagula, 2012, p. 75.)

Kennedy and Zagula go on to suggest many well-known celebrities including actors, actresses, sports figures, business people, doctors, lawyers, and themselves representing finance and copy-writers. They suggest that you can self-publish a book simply with a little effort.

> "You can this as a do-it-yourself project. Most printers can produce a book. You can model

other books for appearance. You can copy-right your book (and other marketing materials) easily and inexpensively via services like LegalZoom.com. And you can get samples..." (No BS, p. 81.)

Self-Publishing

Self-publishing has taken on a new meaning the last couple of years. E-books have emerged as a growing market, and print on demand (pod) has become a more relevant and easier method of producing as little as one book.

There are many tutorials on ***YouTube*** and online that promote e-books and pod books as the up and coming vehicle for publishing books. Amazon Kindle, Smashwords with their "E-readers" and many others are popping up on the internet daily. These can be done at no cost until you sell an eBook. Then Amazon, Smashwords and many others pay you a royalty and keep a commission from each sale.

How to Get the More Results from your Ads

In the book ***How to Make, Market and Sell Ebooks: All For Free.*** by Jason Matthews, the title is somewhat limited. The section covering eBooks is titled "**Formatting and Uploading for Smashwords, Amazon and other Retailers**." (pp. 56-71). Additionally, Matthews covers how to get books printed for free in the section titled, "**Other Things You Can Do**," (pp. 134-135). He lifts up CreateSpace by Amazon and LighteningSource, as sources for self-publishing pod books for free. You as author/publisher pay a small commission per book, and you keep the royalty on each book. (ibid.)

Aventine Press
Book Locker
Book Pros
Create Space by Amazon – The best free place for self-publishing. There are additional fees for add-on services.

Dog Ear Publishing
Infinity Publishing

HEADLINES That Work

Light source

Tate Publishing

Wasteland Press

Xuland Press

WHO NEEDS YOU

Service Organizations

These are often categorized as those that are not-For Profit organizations. These units are typically receiving discounted fees. Some are small and local and others may be national in scope. The smaller variety are represented by little theatre groups, and the larger by the National Organizations or Societies.

A larger organization with statewide or national coverage may surprise you with a large advertising budget. It depends on the scope of the project. It may be difficult to convince their leadership that the headline does not need to include their name. Non-profit does not mean that they have a lean or slim budget.

How to Get the More Results from your Ads

Some headline copywriters spend most of their career working with these organizations; others very seldom do.

Corporations

Hospitals, Utility Districts, Banks, Assisted Living Centers and others can be multiple units or a small standalone. The larger the corporate structure, the more opportunities for the freelance copywriter will be available and needed. There are many departments - customer service, public relations, marketing, technology, training and human relations to name a few. Once you do projects for one department, it is easier to be recommended to the other departments.

The key is letting the department you are working with know the variety of the types of jobs you are capable of doing. A little research can determine what kind of work these corporations need done. Additionally, corporate leadership and high profile people will need assistance in speech development.

HEADLINES That Work

A good place to begin your research is on their web sites. You will usually discover the leadership teams including department heads, email addresses, telephone numbers and even office location.

Associations

These can vary in sizes. The larger ones afford a greater chance for work. These include chambers of commerce, work groups like doctors, lawyers, florists, dentists, carpenters and general contractors. These groups and lobbyists for these groups are potential clients. Most have trade shows or conferences where you can go and meet many possible customers.

Large School Districts - Groups - Clusters

The superintendents or directors are the primary contacts. They need brochures, coursework promotion pieces, public relation materials, maps, logs, web sites, press releases, organizational material, club and sport pieces.

They need help with grant proposals. The size of the district has a bearing on the variety of materials needed.

Colleges and Universities

Whether small town or major metropolitan colleges or universities their needs can provide a very lucrative source of work. Like school districts above they can provide a wide variety of projects. In addition to the types of materials listed above, they will have a need for white papers, articles, postcard copy, email copy, short and long sales letters.

Graphic Designers

This group is diversified as some are freelancers, others run small print shops, managers of large agencies or large print manufacturing facilities, comprise the makeup of said workers. Only the very large concerns will have a staff copywriter, but even those from time to time will get overloaded and need your assistance. Associating with the freelancer and smaller shops will provide a steady income.

Working with the group will provide opportunity for reciprocity. In other words they will give you work and you will return the favor and furnish work for them. Thus, both of you benefit. Teaming up two or three freelance graphic designers can make your life easier. With everyone working together you will spend less time marketing and more time on the finished product.

The relationships you form need to be professional and long lasting. Always do your best. On your side make sure you get everything in on time, and expect the same from them. Make sure your work is free from errors and meets or exceeds their expectations.

At most half of your work will come from this type of team effort. It may be substantially less depending on the type and size of your combined clients. Some clients will have a designer with whom they already work. Some clients associated with graphic designers have copywriters with whom they work.

A team effort usually means a savings for the client and less cost for the team. Usually the person that secured the client, bills for the combined service. Depending on the arrangements between the individuals this may not be the case.

Events, Conferences and Shows

There may be one person in charge with many workers or committee members organizing a huge production together. They may have promotional material they have used in the past; they may not. They may have mailing lists and email lists they contact on a regular basis. Their attendees are used to long sales letters or long emails that provide specific details as well as promotional information.

Speech material is essential, as well as scripting is paramount. Direction and informational brochures are a necessity. Conference references are required in several areas. These are great experiences for a copywriter who hangs around on a regular basis. The person in charge is the person to know. It is possible to develop a series of projects by being around, and being invited to or showing up for meetings.

Sources that are important to check out are arenas, sports facilities and convention centers to find out who is the person in charge.

Marketing, PR and Advertising Agencies

Even the large firms will find themselves needing to supplement their staff with freelance copywriters. The smaller ones will face the need more often. You need to send them a short letter, a brief email or postcard reminding them that you are available when needed. Go by if possible. Leave a sample brochure or effective ad that you created. It may take time before you get noticed.

These agencies are your clients. Your services and fees are between you and them. Keep abreast of business journals and directories, chamber of commerce directories and other listings. (**_The Well-Fed Writer_** by Peter Bowerman. p. 97), 2010.

Finding Clients

Check the medium to larger ads in the newspaper, magazines and local yellow pages. There is a good chance that these advertisers need to hear something unique or new. Trade and association journals, magazines, and papers will give you information about the movers and shakers in that industry. Check web sites, company blogs, articles in the papers, press releases, and local talk shows on TV or radio.

Request referrals after completing an effective project, or doing a job for one department in a medium to large firm. Use your skills to advertise your services. Hold seminars on Headlines with chambers of commerce, or teach a course in Advertising at a local college. If you write a book offer a "how to create an e-book" workshop at a local library.

HEADLINES That Work

Make sure to send out press releases on these events.

Prospecting

Prospecting is the process of getting and making appointments. Do not try to make sales or to make new clients. The uninformed often refer to this as cold calling. In a way they are correct. However, it is not the same as knocking on doors to sell sets of encyclopedias. With reference to presenting your headline or copywriting services, it is a means of being heard.

Being heard can be presented in person or by phone. There are advocates for either method. Even leaving a message with a secretary or on someone's voice mail creates a chance to be heard. Emails, sales letters, postcards and advertising in general enhance the possibility of being heard. Going to meetings are chances to be heard and to be seen.

How to Get the More Results from your Ads

There are times you shout as loud as you can to be heard, and sometimes you find it as effective to speak very softly. The sad thing in prospecting is when you fail to tell your story. At the beginning of your copywriting career this is especially true. Later on you still need to prospect in a lighter way.

Many of you will call this the pre-sale or setting up the appointment. Rarely, you will bump into someone that wants to become a client immediately. When it happens just shout quietly in your heart, "Praise the Lord or Hallelujah."

It will usually take one telephone call or more to make an appointment. The first call will consist of qualifying the potential client by explaining who you are and asking her/him a question, such as, "My name is Le David Morris with DD Images. I do freelance and headline copywriting services. Do you hire or use freelance or headline copywriters?" If the person says yes, go to the next paragraph. If they say no, tell her/him, "I'm sorry to bother you.

Thank you." Then hang up and call the next prospect.

Follow-up calls are reminders that you are still around. These reminders are as important as the original call. Make sure you have a positive outlook with each call.

You may call 10 to 50 businesses before you get one that says, "Yes, we do." Then you ask another question, "Do you have any projects pending?" or you may say, "Would you like to use my services?" Again, they may occasionally say, "Yes." In which you further ask, "What type of projects?"

It may take as many as 1000 to 1500 prospect contacts to get enough interviews. Contacts may stretch out over a few weeks or a few months. It will pay off. Do not worry, you can always fall back on the yellow pages.

They will tell you what projects they have or ask you, "What type of projects do you do?" Your quick response would be, "I do a wide variety of projects.

How to Get the More Results from your Ads

What do you have in mind?" Hopefully, they will tell you at this point.

The prospect may go many different directions with the next statement or question depending on whether it is pricing oriented or possibly about your experience or qualifications. Below is a list:

'Who are you?"

"Tell me about your experience."

"For whom have you worked?"

"How long does it take to do a six panel brochure?"

"Have you ever done an 11" by 17" flyer?"

"Can you send me some samples of your work?"

"How much would you charge for a full page display ad in the local newspaper in full color?"

The above questions are inquiries, not sales. They do not become sales until you have a signed order. A website can answer most of these questions. Some questions can be answered a by simple "yes." Offer to forward the information they need by sending them your website information. Tell them the information they want is on your website and ask for their mail address to send that information to them.

The 30 Second Speech

Many refer to the speech as the 'Elevator Speech' or 'the 30 Second Talk.' It derives its name for the amount of time it takes to tell some who you are and what you do in a typical elevator ride.

That may be all the time you have to exchange business cards and tell each other what you do for a living. Sample dialogue:

Headline copywriter: "I see by your badge, that you are here for the Dolt Conference."

Conference participant: "I'm John, a Dolt participant from this town."

Headline copywriter: "My name is David and I am a freelance copywriter. I do copy for brochures flyers, ad-copy and things similar to that. Does your firm use freelance copywriters?"

How to Get the More Results from your Ads

Conference participant: "Yes we do, but that is not my department. Rita in marketing handles that."

Headline copywriter: "Do you have a card? Here's mine. Do I call this number for Rita?"

They exchange cards. Headline copywriter says, "Have a great conference."

Conference participant: "You too. See you around."

Notice the conversation was simple and natural. The 30 Second Speech needs to be memorized, but adaptable to every encounter. It should tell everyone who you are and what you do. The secret is to tell as many as will listen whether on the phone, by email, regular mail or in person.

Prospecting is not easy for those that have not had to do it before. It is not as bad as we often perceive it. We hate being turned down, rebuffed, or rejected. The wonderful part of prospecting is based on numbers.

HEADLINES That Work

Expert analysts will tell you that 80% of your contacts will reject your offer. The beauty is that means 20% will accept your offer. Out of 500 prospects, 100 will buy the appointment, and half of these will purchase your service.

George

George sold correspondence courses from a university in Illinois. The prospect filled out and sent in a form telling where he/she had an interest in a particular course, such as a high school diploma or a college degree in a specific area.

George was not the typical 22-26 year old selling the courses. He was fiftyish with a previous history in sales. Many of his clients were high school or college dropouts in their early twenties through the late thirties desiring a better chance at life. In a way George was a father figure to the other salesmen and to his clients.

George discovered that the want and the need were usually present, but half of the prospects could not afford the courses. Very early in the presentation he would ask what the person could afford to pay for such a wonderful course that would help them succeed in life. To those that could not afford the courses, he would explain that they needed to wait a little while until they could afford the course or the monthly payments.

His approach netted George top salesman in the St. Louis area, several years in a row, because George came across as someone who cared. George encouraged them to work hard and save their money so they could put a good down payment on the course and budget the monthly payments. Many who could not make the purchase immediately, would call George later. (I was one of those 22 year old sales persons who admired George.)

Believing and caring about the client can be sensed.

Chapter seven tells you some of the places where you can meet people. Other places may be in the grocery line at the store. You may meet others at athletic events or the country club. You may meet someone new working on projects for a volunteer organization.

Anywhere you meet new people will afford the opportunity to share your story. Keep it focused and keep it short. Do not bore people. Then have fun. Talk about anything to build rapport. The numbers are with you, and will not fail you. If you like people, they will like you. If you hear their story, they will listen to you.

You should pre-qualify your prospects by ability, acute need and appealing. First, simply put, can they afford your services? Second, is there an acute need for your services? Third, will it be appealing to purchase your expertise? If you can get an affirmation on these three questions, then the sell will be easy.

After you are known, you will need to do less and less prospecting. You will never get completely away from the possibility that you need to do some prospecting especially when business slows down.

How to Get the More Results from your Ads

Those with a selling background will be used to prospecting. Coming from other backgrounds will cause a feeling of newness to prospecting.

People in business are used to salespersons calling them. They do not take offense like someone at home during supper when a telemarketer calls. Many of them prospect in similar ways. If you do run across a cranky character from time to time, just shake it off and say "sorry to bother you," and hang up.

Using the dialog above as a basis, develop a script. Having words in front of you will help to keep you on tract when you are bombarded with a bunch of questions.

When speaking, speak slowly and deliberately. You will be understood more clearly. Speak cheerfully and politely, but businesslike.

Keep track of your contacts. You will need to note whether it was by phone, in person, email, letter, postcard or other method.

HEADLINES That Work

Selling

People love to buy. However, they do not like to be sold. Your job is to help them make the purchase. (I first read this concept from Jeffrey Gitomer in an email newsletter years ago.) We discussed earlier as a copywriter you are helping clients help their customers to buy. You help your potential clients to buy your services. The more effective you are, at this, the more you are valuable to your clients.

Realize some potential clients will buy, and some will not. If they were pre-qualified in the prospect stage, the chances are they will buy from you. If they do, great. If they do not, that is OK. As stated under prospecting, it is the same with selling, the numbers are with you. You will make one sale out of every two presentations.

Caution, the above information is an average. You may make ten sales in a row and be rejected on the next twelve. Remember it will average out. Once established you will have clients seeking you.

How to Get the More Results from your Ads

If you believe you are going to sell your services, you probably will. Factors may change that you have no control over. Qualifiers may change. They may have found someone else. They may not like the way you smile. Whatever the reason, they might not buy from you. It may be difficult to fathom, but you must refocus on the next call and maintain a positive outlook.

CHAPTER Nine

Secret VII - The Key of Attitude

Considerations

Becoming a freelance copywriter can be rewarding considering the various clients they serve. A good freelance copywriter will make money for their clients and enhance their profit picture. There is satisfaction to be derived from that. Knowing this contributes to your own respect of the field and yourself.

Again, you develop your own timetable. Freelance copywriting permits you to earn an above average income. Family and friends come to respect your working time. You can choose the projects from which you want to work. Variety is unlimited, which keeps you fresh and focused. A specialty of freelance copywriting service is freelance headline writing.

The Thank You Letter

After the decision has been made you must send two types of thank you letters. The first type of thank you letter is to those that decided not to work with you at the present. Simply stated it should say, "Thank you for your time. If I can be of service in the future, feel free to call me. Thanks." Samples to be sent or to be looked at on line are website and other material to be sent including a resume.

The second type of thank you letter is to those who decided to have you work with them. You will want to thank them. Include a copy of the agreement with a schedule for a follow-up meeting, if needed. Don't forget anticipated interviews, or the possibility of one revision.

Beginning the Work through Honest Effort

A client teleconference or face to face meeting may be a matter of choice. It depends on what you and your client feels comfortable doing. Some ways to consider would be a sales call by telephone, Skype or actually seeing the person.

If the sale is confirmed with the client you can move on to the preparatory meeting. If the sale is confirmed later you will need to schedule this prep meeting as quickly as possible.

If you know what the project is going to be, you can gear your samples toward that project. Researching their website and other sources such as brochures, spec sheets, and competitions products that are similar will need to be done.

Discuss the Financial Arrangements

Be upfront and open. If you charge $1200.00 for a six panel brochure that needs to be presented early, You do not want any surprises to pop up at the end of the project. You especially want them to know what you expect.

How to Get the More Results from your Ads

Facilitate your wants by presenting sample prices in sales literature or displayed on your website or blog. Do not accept less. (See chapter Six)

Explore Proximities

What does the client want to benefit from the project?

Who is the competition, and where does your client rate compared to the competition?

Are there any considerations that need to be in the project?

What methods of distribution does the client use?

Who is the client's market, and what turns them on?

How does the client want the project to be used?

Does the client have a motto, phrase or saying with which the market is familiar?

What differentiates your offer from others in the industry?

HEADLINES That Work

Remember you are the expert. Do not get smug or pomp. If you do you will have a tendency to be over-bearing and limit your ability to learn. Maintain a sincere interest and you will surprise yourself with the helpful information you obtain.

In other words be confident, but not overconfident. Demonstrate competence and refrain from being a 'know it all.' Let your client feel you buy into the project.

Courtesy

Call the client the day before to make sure the time is correct. Be early by five to ten minutes. Dress appropriately. Show a few pieces that you have premade or from other projects that would be similar in nature.

The rule is to keep is simple. Also, do not feel insulted if the client has different perceptions for the project.

How to Get the More Results from your Ads

Testimonials and Interviews

Your job as the copywriter is to research infor-mation, or to develop testimonials to contact the client's customers. These individuals should have been referred to you from the client. Often the client will contact these individuals and set up times for phone appointments.

Make sure you follow through. Keep the interviews professional and cordial. Ask the interviewee if it is permissible to record their conversation.

Hiring an Assistant(s)

As your business expands, you will need help. A part time assistant to help with the details of the business, like sending thank you cards, keeping track of scheduling, sending notices can be benefi-cial.

You might want to consider one with some writing ability to teach them to edit, proofread, or even write copy for some simple projects. At times when you find yourself completely overworked, you might consider subbing out your work to another freelance copywriter or headline writer.

The Good Client

The qualities of a good client know the difference between good and bad copywriting. She/he understands timelines, financial arrangements and pays in a timely manner.

The good client presents you with the necessary materials needed for each project. He/she will contact the persons to be interviewed, as well as give you the correct information you need to stay on tract. Clients will provide guidance, but will not over manage the situation. Be able to assist only if needed.

The good client will funnel projects to you whenever the need arises and refer others to you often.

The Bad Client

Beware of controlling clients. Be cautious of the ones who are dictatorial, and the ones with low budgets. Smaller clients are more restrictive.

How to Get the More Results from your Ads

Watch out for those that over edit and want to interject bad copy into your work. Some believe they can write when they have no idea what good writing is.

The client that is not experienced with copywriting, or even good writing can draw on your time and patience.

Titles of Articles and Books Speak as Headlines

The title speaks volumes in that it attract readers. Subtitles expand the title like it is part of a headline. The reader is drawn by the title alone. If the title is startling, steamy, exotic, instructive, or explosive it will attract readers. Most titles are short but powerful. The title often reveals the content, audience and the gain or benefit. In other words the same criteria for a good headline.

Millions of books have been sold based on the title. A title delivers a clear and effective message of the benefit of the article, book, white paper, CD or video.

HEADLINES That Work

More on Articles

Articles from 400 to 700 words can help build your credibility. In high school most students learn the five paragraph method of writing essays - one way to write a type of article that is believable and achievable. Many flounder when first starting to write. With a little practice a beginner can polish their style and flair. You may want to rely on your essay experience to assist you in writing articles. Writing articles helps to build your credibility in your writing. They draw good prospects to your landing page or send them to your store, shop or clinic. Clients will pay you to write them for and about the products and services. You can write a variety of article styles with minor adjustments.

Each article should get your reader to ponder and believe your message with excitement. Achievement is conquered by directing the message toward an emotion of understanding, appreciation, or choice you desire them to receive.

How to Get the More Results from your Ads

Writing an article is similar to writing good sales copy. You want to focus on the direction of your article. Writers are called to fascinate and enrich their audience with articles. They also provide information to assist their readers to correct or to purchase something.

From the beginning you have to sense the direction the article is taking. You need to make sure the message moves toward that goal. The reader must think "wow, I can and will do this."

Develop a sketch on how the article will assist the readers to make up their minds. Specifying the advantages of the resultants or offering of your making in direct mail piece is a must. It is paramount in aiding you to create the article. Three to five advantages will be relevant in the article to make it worth reading.

More than six advantages perhaps may cause confusion, disinterest and disorientation. Begin with the major advantage in the first paragraph and end with the rephrased version of the same advantage in the last paragraph.

Reveal Pertinent Results

Teach your reader the results of presented advantages. You will need to inspire her/ him as a result. Revealing could be as plain as demonstrating how easy the product or service operates.

Relate to the Reader

You connect with your reader. You should desire for your reader to relate to the advantages discovered in your article.

In your article, the reader identifies with the piece by thinking about the next time he prices an assignment. All he has to do is get his foot in the door with a client, and then follow my instructions for offering a package. He can actually see it happening to him.

How to Get the More Results from your Ads

Anticipate Doubts or Misgivings

The crucial part is relative toward reviewing and revising your writing. Disclosing obvious fear or distrust and dealing with it honestly will propel your writing. Sincerely list common objections. Then simply answer them in your article. Do not overemphasize the inquiry. Assure the reader is satisfied.

Direct Mail Pieces

What is more often referred to as sales letters come in the short and long variety. Advocates for either can be counted in large numbers on either side. Many opt for a compromise and say it depends on the writer. Dan S. Kennedy author of ***The Ultimate Sales Letter*** encourages those who embrace the larger format and has made a fortune creating long sales letters (see above.)

You will hear the phrase, "content is King." This indicates the copy used in the sales letter must hold the reader's attention, but the reader must be mesmerized and motivated by the message. The headline sets the tone and both begins and summarizes that message. In actuality headlines are the authentic "King." The headline has to captivate the recipient to move through to the next line and to next line and moves the reader on to the next and so on.

A sales letter that is carefully designed with tremendous motivational material can guide a reader to make a purchase. It all begins with the headlines encouraging to pursue the content, sub headlines or paragraph titles.

Many are attracted by the envelope as it provokes their curiosity.

Direct mail pieces whether long, short or even postcards, possess the elements below. These same elements have been presented previously. Thus, just a few words or a sentence at most will be presented to help refresh your memory.

How to Get the More Results from your Ads

1. Consider style and detail.

2. Lead the reader to make a decision.

3. Distinguish the copy with subheads, paragraph titles, bullets—Say it again! Say it again! Say the message in several different ways.

4. Focus on your reader.

5. Lift up the greatest advantage, along with some other major advantages—benefits versus features.

Emails That Slap Them in the Face

Email subject lines have to, "Slap them in the Face," or wake your readers up. You have a phrase or at the most a short sentence to grab someone's attention to get them to open the email. You have three to five words before someone hits the delete button. You may have the greatest content that has ever been written, but if it is never read it does not make a difference.

HEADLINES That Work

Do not put the words in the subject line in caps. The recipient will think she/he has gotten spam and will delete the email.

Earlier stated in this book was the fact that you have a few seconds to gain a person's interest. In emails you do not have that. In a fraction of a second they make up their mind to dump you or to see if you have something they will want to read. If you can not arouse them, woo them, shock them, startle them, encourage them, enrage them, or excite them to read more they are gone.

You really do not have time to develop a relationship with the reader. It is more like creating "love at first sight." The key is if they love your introductory words, they will want to love your writing. Once they open the email, then the few second rule applies, which results in further exploration.

If you want to keep them reading you now evoke passion and warm compassion in the first sentence or two in the email. Hereby there is now an extension to the reference line, similar to a headline or a

How to Get the More Results from your Ads

sub headline. You should now be assisted in better reaction toward the content or the message and ultimately to achieve greater response at the end of the email.

Personal, Friendly, and Up close

Treat the reader like a friend because she/he is. In fact they are closer than many friends; they are important enough to share your secrets. You can share the things that bug you as well as the ones that excite you and make you happy.

Your mood and emotion will be sensed from the depth of your being making you appear authentic. Is this not the way most people communicate with friends, family and close co-workers? Your emails should emit the same conversational expectation.

When the reader believes your sincerity and you are not pushing a sales message on her/him they will stay with you. Remember in sales basics that the proposed client wants to buy and they love to buy. One might go as far as to say they live to buy, but they do not like, nor do they want, to be sold. Thus, it is your duty to help them buy your product or service.

The first thing the reader can sense about your writing is if you care about them. Do you project that caring and concern in your message? If you do they will pick up on that. They do want to know the reason you are sending them a particular message, and how it will benefit them. You do want to create emotional depth from your offer to help them from your email message.

Your goal is to have your reader feeling like you understand them. You want them to think: "Said person is on my side, and wants to help."

Do you possess conviction in what you write? You have seen many emails that are out and totally unbelievable. They are sent by either senders that do not believe in what they are writing, or they are sent by those that are working a con and do not care. Emails that attract attention and cause people to affirm or buy receive the message from one who truly desires writing about the things in which they believe.

Emails that have impressed you in the past are good models to use. Study them for style, content, and passion. Use the best of these to model your own writing. Write the email, with the reader or audience in mind **and not the writer.**

You always have to focus on to who you are writing regardless of the content. You are basically writing to one person. Make the message about your reader and the benefit she/he will receive. Using the second tense may be difficult. It is easy to fall into the first or third when writing.

It becomes difficult to keep a personal story from creeping through, but you must realize the reader wants to know how it helps her/him. Remember the reader uses the call letters WIIFM: "What's in it for me?" or "Why if it's NOT for me why should I read your email?" What is the reader's major concern? What turns them on?

HEADLINES That Work

Remember, the reader needs to recognize very early on that the email he's reading is about him. You (the writer) are trying to help him solve a problem, or obtain some benefit. So, make sure he sees that right away.

Write to a Particular Individual

Writing like you are speaking to one person is a good idea and may appear apparent. The previous statement is true for all headlines and copywriting, but it is disregarded many times in writing emails. The rule is you never write for a big group or audience. You write to that one reader about whom you care. (Refer to comments above.)

Example: **"If you're concerned about your mortgage call ABBMC"**

Do not write an email from a group. When writing for a large organization, send it in the name of the president or one representative of that organization. It is easier to relate with one person.

How to Get the More Results from your Ads

Concentrate on the Greatest Benefit or Value.

Numerous good benefits can make it difficult to decipher the greatest benefit. Many good copywriters wander at times. If many concepts or benefits are floating around in an email, it is difficult for the reader to remain focused and concentrate on your writing. If you keep your focus your reader will keep hers/his. Keep to that one choice directed objective, perceptive point, or in which you choose to draw the reader.

Remember to write your subject line or header to match your copy. The writer needs to duplicate the ideas of header with the content. Make sure it is a single concept or benefit.

Sophia's Call

EPILOGUE

The last chapter is a mixture of insights and a desire to keep the book real. Drawing on the wisdom of the ages with reference to headlines we hope to avoid the vagueness of the esoteric, and present that which elucidates or lights up the wisdom of the common sense. Hopefully, the seven keys will afford the enlightenment to produce that reality.

The Language

You will notice the change in language in the catch up section. I will transition from second person single to first person. My story is intermingled throughout the book directed at you the reader. The emphasis is on you. It was difficult to keep from injecting myself in the body of this work.

How to Get the More Results from your Ads

I can justify the transition because what I share in this last section explores what has worked for me specifically.

It is Great for Me

Freelance headline writing and freelance copywriting are lucrative ventures with ponderous choices that are enjoyable with a passion. Ambition and helping others will provide satisfaction. Learning how a few markets work makes one appear as an expert. Enjoying writing and speaking gives you a feeling of achievement. There is a desperate need for good writers.

Hopefully writing the book will inspire readers to become good at copywriting – specifically specializing in headline writing. It is a beautiful career to pursue.

No Defeats

Since the stroke December 18, 2010, I have been a different person in physical and mental ability. Physical ability has been diminished by limitation in walking and driving. Not only have I lost about 200 pounds, but somehow I have lost about five inches in height.

Mental ability is about the same. I have a similar capacity for absorbing information by listening and reading. However, I find myself more emotional and tear up at old sad movies, I am easily provoked to anger, but am doing great today with some minor limitations.

Diversified with Help

You may ask, "With teaching, preaching, and running a screen-printing business and operating a freelance copywriting service, when did you have time for anything else?" The simple answer is - I have used assistants or aides for years. They have kept me going.

I have also used outside trainers and other freelancers from time to time. It made the business easier to manage and to keep within a controllable timeframe.

How to Get the More Results from your Ads

Both Worlds

Insurance coverage and security in regular everyday jobs provided a base and copywriting produced extra income in freelance work, resulting in the best of both worlds for me.

Copywriting in All Jobs

Copywriting ability has helped supplement every job. Having a limited knowledge of graphic design and desktop publishing has helped immensely and contributed to the work as a copywriter.

Volunteer Organizations

At different times I was able to serve in the Lions Club, Rotary, Civitan and the JAYCEES and was President of our local teachers union. Through these clubs and organizations many contacts were made on the state and national levels. Not intentionally promoting copywriting skills has led to developing promotional pieces for every organization individuals within the groups served. I did not join these organizations to sell my services. However, they were great for meeting new friends and learning my way around in new communities where services were needed.

Do not be shy about offering services. Let it be known what services you possess. Let it be known in a casual way that you do copywriting in preparing brochures, posters and flyers at no charge for the organization. Ultimately a business owner or a corporation president will approach about doing the same type of work for her/his business. Over the years clientele developed very quietly with very little marketing effort, and at a very low marketing cost.

Low Cost Marketing

Most everything in marketing can be low cost and low effort. Occasionally, sending out a hundred sales letters or flyers created using desktop publishing techniques will produce excellent results. Response can be as much as 10%. You will have to do very little prospecting in your later years.

How to Get the More Results from your Ads

In the earlier stages of securing business a lot of cold calls may have to be made. Meaning going into a business or office and announcing yourself and asking to talk to the person in charge. If she/he was in? Announce again who you are to that person and what your services are, and then ask if he/she uses your type of services. If they did, offer to present some samples or make an appointment for a later time. If they did not, give them your card. Thank them for allowing you to speak to them, shake hands and depart.

About twice a week someone would buy services from those cold calls. Using these techniques should produce several appointments every month and several phone calls to make appointments within two weeks of cold calls.

Printing Process

In those earlier years making contact with a local printer or graphic designer will help produce completed projects for clients. Many printers will not use the title graphic designer, but are very capable of finishing most pieces created. Graphic designers are the optimal choice.

Even though many print shops have the skills needed, with the preponderance of wonderful graphic designers it becomes a three tier process - the copywriter, the graphic designer, and the printer. With modern printing processing the finished project comes along a lot faster.

Plenty of Work

I live in the relatively small region outside of Jackson, Tennessee called the Golden Circle. Memphis is a little over an hour, and Nashville is around two hours away. With up-to-date internet service, scanner-printer-fax-copy machines, a fairly fast computer and a cell phone I have access to the world. I communicate with friends in Thailand as quickly as the person next door.

With the resources that I have available it is easy to attract clients from anywhere. There is a market

How to Get the More Results from your Ads

for those that have the interest. It does take initiative and hard work, but the reward is an above average income. Your income can range between $75.00 - $150.00 an hour.

Social Media

I love social media and have been on LinkedIn for two years, but did not make use of it until two months ago. Been working with Facebook, LinkedIn, and Google+ for about an hour a day for two months except one evening three weeks ago. It was mesmerizing to get caught in every ones conversations with five hours passing without realizing it. During the past two months I have made over 2000 contacts, friends and connections. It is easy to see how one writer made thousands of connections from all over the world working forty hours a week for a month. Essentially inform these supporters of the service of or book that is being launched.

HEADLINES That Work

One out of Twenty Will

Probably one out of twenty that reads this book will act on the information. I have lived the life and know it works. It is not a get rich scheme, but can be very rewarding. The choice is yours. I hope the stories help you in your decision.

The Last Two Years

The first year after the stroke was depressing and I wasted a lot of time watching television all hours of the day. The second year was spent reading ferociously, and learning two languages – Spanish and Thai. Starting the third year has meant launching four websites, and writing three books. Presently a forth book is forming with a fifth one in mind.

Some would think that this old man needs to sit back and be quiet. There are those that believe older people are through in life and do not have anything to contribute. Many of us know that life is beginning again when we get older. Something motivates us to keep going. I do not want anybody to feel sorry for me - most everything is alright. I have limitations on walking and driving, but praise God I am still alive. Death has been cheated and I can dance in my mind.

Last Words

I was munching on a small cheeseburger and salad from the dollar menu at a local restaurant last week. A friend was sitting at the table next to me. We were chatting about my losing in excess of 200 pounds since the stroke. A lady two tables over asked me how I lost the weight. I told her that someone at the hospital told me if I did not lose a substantial amount of weight that I would die. I continued to tell her that for the next six months I went on a fear diet, and lost most of that weight. She told me she had a son who weighed over 350 pounds - hoping he would listen to one that almost died. She looked at me with a pleading look and said that I needed to write a book. I told her I was thinking about doing that very thing. She asked me what the title was going to be. I blurted out, not thinking, "How to Lose 200 Pounds to Survive and Live." She said she would buy it to give to her son. Thus, my to do list includes a book which is not on paper, but has already has one customer. What better motivation?

If I can help one person make a decision, I have reached my goal as a writer. My advice is to do it. It does not make a difference whether you do it full time or part time. It will not be easy at first, but it will over time.

Read the books that are included in "Suggested Reading." These books in addition to this one will help train and prepare you for the life and life style as a Freelance Headline Copywriter. Join an organization like American Writers and Artist Incorporated (AWAI.) They will help give you the training you need.

Suggested Reading

Checking These Out

"***The 250 Power Words that Sell***." by Stephen Schiffman.

"***No B. S. Trust Base Marketing: The Ultimate Guide to Creating Trust in an Understandably Un-Trusting World***" by Dan S. Kennedy and Matt Zagula.

"***A Copywriter's Handbook***" by Robert Bly. A book that answers many basic questions and helps in honing copywriting skills; it is particularly useful for the copywriting novice. He has also authored many books.

"***The Elements of Copywriting***" and an updated version of Bly's handbook, which deals with the world of the web.

"***The Everything Guide to Writing Copy***" by Steve Saunwhite. I enjoyed and learned from this work. Elementary concepts of what freelance copywriting should be.

HEADLINES That Work

"***The Online Copywriter's Handbook.***" by Dan Kennedy. Another great resource. He has also authored several valuable books.

"***How to Make, Market and Sell Ebooks, All for FREE,***" 2010 by Jason Matthews. Jason's work inspired me to self-publish this book on Amazon's Kindle and the printed version on Create Space.

"***Outrageous Advertising That's Outrageously Successful***." by Bill Glazer.   A book that is entertaining and powerful. It is directed to small businesses who want a better return on their advertising. It is autobiographical and full of Glazer's successful ads.

"***Teach Yourself Copywriting***" by J. Jonathan Gabey is another good volume to consider.

"***The Wealthy Freelancer: 12 Secrets to a Great Income and an Enviable Lifestyle***." by Steve Slaunwhite, Pete Savage, and Ed Gandia. They bring a wealth of knowledge to motivate and encourage you to join the ranks of freelance copywriters.

"***The Well-Fed Writer***," by Peter Bowerman. The best presentation on the subject of freelance copywriting. It will have you laughing one moment and crying the next. It is easy to read, but the content is rich and powerful. Bower-man presents the essence of commercial freelance copy-writing in an autobiographical format that is intriguing. He uses the term Freelance Commercial Writer. He is the only writer I know that uses that term when referring to Free-lance Copywriters. One can become immersed in the story and the content. Bowerman is my favorite author.

"***The Writer's Market***," which is published annually, provides potential companies to contact; its yearly salary section also provides a larger picture of the market. As mentioned before, a good style book and thesaurus are ad-ditional essentials for this job.

"***The Ultimate Sales Letter.***" by Dan S. Kennedy. The focus on long sales letters, but applicable to a wide array of freelance copywriting skills. Kennedy is a marketing guru in the freelance copywriting industry. His influence spans small and very large businesses. He commands and re-ceives exceptionally large fees for his services. Kennedy has published many books. He advocates publishing to gain the appearance as an expert and for creating trust and ac-ceptance in business and industry.

Check out the follow Job leads for Memberships that are worth the price.

American Association of Advertising Agencies

HEADLINES That Work

Association of Freelance Copywriters

American Marketing Association

You're local **Chamber of Commerce**. The relationships you develop with business leaders make wonderful contacts.

Online Sources for Securing Job Leads – Their forums and chat rooms are helpful.

Craigslist

Freelance Job Openings

Journalism Jobs

Media Bistro

Online Writing Jobs

How to Get the More Results from your Ads

INDEX

26 Headlines – Formulas, Suggestions an Working Models That are Powerful... 45

80% Will Read the Headlines 25

9 Steps That Influence Headlines to Empower 33

A Copywriter or an Ad-person 59

An Introduction to Independent Ad-writing 1

Anticipate Doubts or Misgivings 118

Associations.......................... 89

Beginning the Work through Honest Effort 108

Bonus – Intervention – Overcome Obstacles 43

Born and Bred for Advertising................................3

Both Worlds........................ 130

CHAPTER Eight...................... 75

CHAPTER Five 33

CHAPTER Four 23

CHAPTER Nine 107

Chapter One 1

CHAPTER Seven 59

CHAPTER Six 45

CHAPTER Three 17

CHAPTER Two................................9

Colleges and Universities 90

Concentrate on the Greatest Benefit or Value. 126

Considerations 107

Copywriting in All Jobs 130

Corporations 88

Courtesy.. 111

Desktop Publishing and Design xi

Direct Mail Pieces 118

Diversified with Help 129

Do not Limit Your Expectations 72

Doing It Wrong v

Eight – Impassioned - Headlines Unfurl Emotion............................... 42

EIGHT: The Secret of (writing an EBook.).. 49

EIGHTEEN: Here's a Quick Way to (Eliminate an Annoyance) 53

ELEVEN: See How Easily You Can (design a bookcover for publishing your book.) 50

EPILOGUE...................................... 127

Events, Conferences and Shows ... 92

How to Get the More Results from your Ads

Explore Proximities............110

Fees...68

FIFTEEN: The Lazy (Women's) Way to (Writing a Novel.) 52

Finding Clients.......................94

Five – Irresistible - Action Potent Words 39

FIVE: THE 10 TOP THINGS YOU CAN DO TO ENHANCE YOUR RETIREMENT..........................48

Four - Inclined - Headlines have to Propel Action 38

FOUR: Who Else Wants (a Greater Salary?) 47

FOURTEEN: Get Rid of (This Problem) Once and For All ...52

Freelancing 59

George 101

Going into Business as a Freelance Copywriter 62

Graphic Designers 90

Headlines Do Not Come Easy 26

Headlines Draw You In 26

Hiring an Assistant(s)..........112

It is Great for Me.................128

Jobs-Freelance-Copywriters.66

Large School Districts - Groups - Clusters 89

Last Words......................................136

Local Places for Freelance Copywriters......................................68

Low Cost Marketing.....................131

Marketing...75

Marketing, PR and Advertising Agencies 93

More on Articles 115

Nine - Igniting – Headlines that Generate Excitement......................42

NINE: Here is a Method that is Helping (business) to (keep more profit)...49

NINETEEN: Now You Can (have Favorable Outcomes) (with Wonderful Results)........................54

No Defeats.....................................128

One – Improvement – Make It Better...33

One out of Twenty Will 135

ONE: If you're (a frequent traveler,) you can (save 50% on your travel.) 46

One-Half – Alliteration 33

P.T Barnum Advertiser Extraordinaire 17

Personal, Friendly, and Up close .122

Places to Work as Freelance

HEADLINES That Work

Copywriter 67

Plenty of Work 133

PREFACE v

Press Releases 80

Printing Process 132

Prospecting 95

Reveal Pertinent Results ... 117

Screen-printing Success with FREE Offer 14

Secret I - The Key of Attraction 9

Secret II - The Key of Attention 17

Secret III - The Key of Attainment 23

Secret IV - The Key of Approach 33

Secret IV Continued - The Key of Approach 45

Secret V - The Key of Alignment 59

Secret VI - The Key of Audience 75

Secret VII - The Key of Attitude 107

Self-Publishing 85

Selling 105

Service Organizations 87

Seven – Invaluable -Headlines Reflect Worth 41

SEVEN: How (this obvious mistake) made Me (Rich.) 49

SEVENTEEN: Design your own T-Shirts Online Quickly and Inexpensively Using our FREE Templates. 53

Six – Inventive- Headlines Evoke Inspiration 41

SIX: I lost 213 lbs. Using This Dynamic Method. 48

SIXTEEN: If You Don't (do it) Now, You'll Hate Yourself Later. 52

Social Marketing 77

Social Media 134

Some More Marketing Tips.......... 79

Sophia's Call 127

Stay-At-Home Mom...................... 20

Stumbled into Freelance Copywriting 5

Suggested Reading 138

TEN: Warning: (three out of five office workers will lose their jobs in the next five years.) 50

Testimonials and Interviews 112

The 30 Second Speech 99

The Bad Client 113

The Call to Copywriting 26

The Few Seconds Rule 25

The Good Client 113

The Good, the Bad and the Indifferent vii

How to Get the More Results from your Ads

The Grocer's Headline 14

The Last Two Years 135

The Purpose of Headlines 12

The Story 9

THIRTEEN: Do You Recognize the (5) Early Warning Signs of (a Stroke?) 51

Three –Infinitesimal - Keep the Headline Short 36

THREE: Tennessee Woman Discovers a Simple method to make 1.4 Million Dollars in Six Months With Less Than $15.00 Investment. 47

Titles of Articles and Books Speak as Headlines 114

TWELVE: Little Known Ways to (cooling your home and saving money.)...................................51

TWENTY: Making Magnificent and Majestic Proclamations.54

TWENTY-FIVE: What Everybody Ought to Know About (buying classy cloths) 56

TWENTY-FOUR: Are You (Wishing You had a Better Job?)......................................56

TWENTY-ONE: (Take Action) like (an Authority Figure) 55

TWENTY-SIX: Straightforward or Basic Headlines................57

TWENTY-THREE: Have a (or) Build a (House) You Can Be Proud Of 56

TWENTY-TWO: Promote the "How-to" Longing 55

Two – Impact - The Headline Must Influence...34

TWO: (Four) Ways to (lose 30 Pounds in 30 days.).........................46

Volunteer Organizations 130

Who Can Write Capable Headlines...23

WHO NEEDS YOU 87

Write and Publish a Book...............84

Write to a Particular Individual ...125

Writing for the Internet 29

www.ingramcontent.com/pod-product-compliance
Lightning Source LLC
Chambersburg PA
CBHW070929210326
41520CB00021B/6861